CAMBRIDGE LATIN AMERICAN STUDIES

47

CAPITALIST DEVELOPMENT AND THE PEASANT ECONOMY IN PERU

*For a list of other books in the
Cambridge Latin American Studies series,
please see page 141*

CAPITALIST DEVELOPMENT AND THE PEASANT ECONOMY IN PERU

ADOLFO FIGUEROA

Professor of Economics
Catholic University of Peru

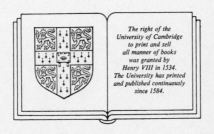

The right of the
University of Cambridge
to print and sell
all manner of books
was granted by
Henry VIII in 1534.
The University has printed
and published continuously
since 1584.

CAMBRIDGE UNIVERSITY PRESS

Cambridge
London   New York   New Rochelle
Melbourne   Sydney

Published by the Press Syndicate of the University of Cambridge
The Pitt Building, Trumpington Street, Cambridge CB2 1RP
32 East 57th Street, New York, NY 10022, USA
296 Beaconsfield Parade, Middle Park, Melbourne 3206, Australia

First published 1984

Printed in Great Britain at the University Press, Cambridge

Library of Congress catalogue card number: 83–18861

British Library Cataloguing in Publication Data
Figueroa, Adolfo
Capitalist development and the peasant economy in
Peru.–(Cambridge Latin American studies; 47)
1. Poor–Peru   2. Peru–Economic conditions
I. Title
339.4'6'0985   HC260.P6

ISBN 0 521 25397 7

TM

To IVAN and ROCÍO

Contents

Tables

viii

Figures

Acknowledgments

This book summarizes much of my research work of the last five years. I initiated the study of the peasant economy in Peru in 1976, thanks to a grant from the Social Science Research Council. The bulk of the study on peasant communities was done within the ECIEL Program (Estudios Conjuntos de Integración Económica Latino-americana) and financed by the Inter American Development Bank through a *convenio* with ECIEL, during 1978–9. I must also acknowledge the financial sources utilized during 1977–9 from the grants given to the Economics Department, Catholic University, by the Ford Foundation and the Canadian International Development Agency. The University of Illinois at Urbana-Champaign provided me with computational assistance during my stay at the Economics Department as visiting professor in 1980.

Juan Ccamapaza, Wilfredo Ccori, Oscar Chaquilla, Jorge Díaz, Matilde Ladrón de Guevara, Felix Olaguivel, Ramiro Oregón, Cirilo Quispitupa, Zoilo Quispitupa and Aurelio Succa, participated in the fieldwork. In the stage of computational work I was assisted by Bruno Barletti, Augusto Cáceres, Jorge Rojas, Mario Tello and Edgar Norton (at the University of Illinois). They all did an excellent job and I am very grateful to them. Special thanks must go to María Gabriela Vega and Daniel Cotlear who helped me efficiently in all the stages of the research.

Many friends gave me valuable comments and suggestions at different stages of the study. I received great intellectual support from the ECIEL Program. Philip Musgrove, the technical coordinator of the group, checked the analytics of the study on communities, and the other members of the group, Alberto Petrecolla, Héctor Dieguez, Jorge Rodríguez, Mauricio Carrizosa and John Elac (from the Inter American Development Bank), were always interested in the economic and social problems of the peasantry of my country. Werner

Baer and the late Robert Ferber, at the University of Illinois, contributed valuable comments to my work.

David Lehmann, Thomas Reardon, Alain Threffersen, Melissa Birch and Russ Smith were generous enough to help me not only with ideas and comments but also with translations and improvements in the presentation of my ideas in English. Chapters 2–6 were published in Spanish by the Catholic University as *La Economía Campesina de la Sierra del Perú* (Lima, 1981). I also thank the two anonymous referees provided by Cambridge University Press for their comments.

I would also like to thank my colleagues and my students of the Economics Department, at the Catholic University in Lima, for their encouragement. Javier Iguiñiz, Head of the Department, helped me in many ways to get this book published. Carmen Rosa Polo made an excellent job of typing the manuscript.

This study could never have been done without the help of the peasant communities studied. My gratitude to them is enormous; and my commitment to the solution of peasant poverty is even greater. I only hope that this book can contribute to the correct understanding of the problem.

Lima
November 1982

1

Introduction

Peasant families represent approximately 25% of the population in Latin America. They get their family income mostly from their small plots of land. Despite the undoubted importance of peasant economies, there are as yet no satisfactory accounts or explanations of their economic functioning and dynamics. The peasant economy constitutes a 'reality without a theory'.

The importance of the peasantry comes not only from the number of people but also from the fact that they represent the poorest social group in Latin America. Several studies have shown that poverty in Latin America is concentrated in rural areas and particularly in the peasant families. Inequality and poverty will continue to be an unfortunate characteristic of this region unless the real incomes of peasant families are increased substantially. Economic policy to reduce poverty must have the peasantry as one of the most important target groups. Policies without theory however will not be successful, except by accident. Again, our understanding of this particular reality becomes a necessity.

This study is concerned with the peasant economy of Peru. This country presents one of the extreme cases of inequality and rural poverty in Latin America. Also the peasant population in Peru is a large fraction of the total population (around 30%) and of the rural population (around 66%). The historical process has, on the other hand, generated in Peru one of the most extreme cases of cultural duality, if one compares the sierra peasants and the upper and middle classes living in Lima. Nowhere else does the notion of economic duality seem more applicable than in Peru.

The scope of the study includes the analysis of the functioning of the peasant economy in its present historical form in Peru, that is, in the context of a predominantly capitalist system. The specific forms that the economic and social relations between the peasantry and the

1

rest of the economy take are the central issues in this study. From the understanding of these relations, the role of the peasant economy in the entire economic system can be better analyzed. The changes in that role over time are also part of the scope of the study.

The method of investigation consists of studying in great detail a sample of peasant communities in the most traditional and backward region of Peru, the southern sierra. The fieldwork lasted about four years (1976–9) and, in addition to questionnaires to collect quantitative data, an anthropological approach was used in order to understand processes and collect more qualitative data, particularly on economic rationality. The results of this study of communities constitute the core of the empirical data used in the analysis. However, secondary sources have also been utilized at several points in the book.

Investigating the case of Peru has a great methodological value for the understanding of the peasant economy in Latin America. Because this study refers to a case of extreme dualism in Latin America, some results will apply with greater force to the general case in Latin America. For instance, if our empirical research shows that the degree of economic integration is significant in the case of Peru, the conclusion to be drawn is that the peasant economy is an integral part of the economic system in Peru, but this degree of integration is much higher in the general case of Latin America. Other results of our study will enhance the understanding of the peasant economy in other individual countries.

The book is divided into nine chapters. Chapter 2 presents the hypotheses about rural poverty in Peru and Latin America, which set the questions to be answered in the study. A framework of analysis is then constructed. This framework has been applied to the study of the peasant communities in the southern sierra region of Peru. As indicated above, this region is one of the poorest and most 'traditional' rural areas in Peru and in Latin America, and the study of this reality has also a methodological value. Chapters 3–6 present the results of the research in those peasant communities. Chapters 7 and 8 place the peasant economy in dynamic context, within the Peruvian experience, with economic growth since 1950 and economic crisis since 1975 respectively. Chapter 9 contains some conclusions in terms of the hypotheses on rural underdevelopment, the dynamics of the peasant economy under capitalist development in Peru, and the economic policies that the case studies suggest.

2

Scope and method

Hypotheses on peasant economies

The persistence of poverty in the peasant economy in Latin America calls for an explanation. For this, the study of the functioning of the peasant economy and its relation to the rest of the economic system is required. In fact, the relevant hypotheses can be classified according to the emphasis given either to the production process or to the process of exchange as the main cause of the economic backwardness of the peasantry.

The production process

There are two common views concerning peasant economies: (1) they are inefficient in their use of resources; (2) they are over-populated, due to the absence of capitalist rules of production and distribution. Against these two hypotheses, Professor Theodore Schultz (1964) has developed a new proposition in terms of 'traditional agriculture'. His hypothesis is basically the following: there is no significant inefficiency or overpopulation in peasant economies. Poverty here can be explained by the poor quality of resources and the traditional technology in use. Peasant families are poor but efficient. As he put it: 'the community is poor because the factors on which the economy is dependent are not capable of producing more under existing circumstances. Conversely, ... the observed poverty is not a consequence of any significant inefficiencies in factor allocation' (p. 48).

In a dynamic sense, Schultz argues that 'the factors of production on which a community depends are expensive sources of economic growth' (p. 97). This is to say that the rate of return of traditional capital is very low. The peasant economy is highly endowed with traditional factors of production; the idea that there is scarcity of capital in this economy and that the rate of return should then be very high has no empirical base : the stock of traditional capital is very high and, consequently, the rate of return very low. Moreover, this low rate of return does not create incentives to save and invest in those factors. The policy implication of this hypothesis is that the peasant economy should shift to the use of modern factors of production.

Another hypothesis refers to the land tenure system. According to this view, peasant families are exploited through non-capitalist social relations, like share-cropping systems. These systems of production and distribution would also have negative effects on the propensities to introduce innovations and technical change in the production process. A land reform program would be the policy to follow based on this hypothesis.

The process of exchange

With regard to the exchange process, there are two conflicting hypotheses. The first says that the peasant economy is not sufficiently integrated into the rest of the economic system. This is the well-known hypothesis of 'economic dualism'. The peasant economy is basically a self-sufficient economy, outside the market system. Therefore, the economic growth that takes place in the capitalist sector does not spread to the peasantry due to the lack of linkages between these two sub-systems.

The second hypothesis suggests exactly the contrary. The peasant economy is well integrated into the capitalist economy through the market mechanism and, therefore, the peasant family is subject to the system of exploitation of capitalism. It is due to this integration that the peasant economy becomes an underdeveloped economy (de Janvry, 1974).

In order to test empirically the explanatory power of these hypotheses, the process of production and exchange in peasant economies must be studied. The particular reality which will be studied for this purpose are the peasant communities of the sierra region of Peru. The required analytical framework, which incorporates the basic elements of this reality, is presented below.

The analytical framework

Technological and market relations

The peasant community is not only an aggregate of families but a social context which establishes certain economic relationships among its members, and in which certain economic decisions are reached collectively and certain economic activities are carried out collectively. It is, indeed, the macroeconomic framework of the peasant family which is the basic economic unit. As such, it comprises three sectors of production: agricultural goods (A), livestock (P), and a wide range of non-agricultural goods such as crafts, processed foods, and construction which we shall call 'Z-goods' (Hymer and Resnick, 1969). This mix of activities is found in most cases, although, to be sure, there are also cases of specialization in potato production, in pastoral activity, and in weaving.

In order to undertake production, the community possesses two primary factors of production – land (T) and labor (H) – and three types of initial stocks of products which correspond to the three sectors mentioned above: seed (A), animals (P) and tools (Z). These goods are produced, but since 'one needs commodities to produce commodities', they must be already available as initial stocks if production is to be undertaken. Other inputs enter into the production of A, P and Z-goods, as flows, and they come either from the community's annual production or from its imports. The community as a whole exchanges with two 'external sectors': the rest of the rural economy (N) (other communities and haciendas) and the urban economy (M).

A table of 'intersectoral relations' (Table 2.1) offers an analytical approach to the relationships between primary factors of production, initial stocks of goods and inputs on the one hand, and the annual product and its allocation on the other. In Table 2.1 the agricultural production of a particular year is represented by X_1. This product is *net* in the sense that it excludes the seed used, and it is allocated as inputs to the same year's cattle production (e.g. as oats, barley and other animal feeds), and to the production of Z-goods (the inputs being processed into food, such as potatoes to be dehydrated for *chuño*, and maize for beer, *chicha*). The remainder of the agricultural production is for consumption (C_1), for the accumulation of further stocks for the subsequent agricultural production cycle (I_1) and for export or sale outside the community (N_1 and M_1).

A year's livestock production is represented by X_2. It comprises: the number of animals produced, including chickens and guinea-pigs; derivative products, such as milk, eggs, wool and skins; and dung, which is used as fertilizer. Part of the production from this sector is dedicated to the productive process as inputs: fertilizer for agriculture; inputs for Z-good production (e.g. milk for cheese, wool

Table 2.1 *Intersectoral relations in the economy of a peasant community*

		Sectors			Consumption	Investment	Exports		
		A	P	Z	C	I	N	M	Total
Agricultural goods	A	0	X_{12}	X_{13}	C_1	I_1	N_1	M_1	X_1
Livestock	P	X_{21}	0	X_{23}	C_2	I_2	N_2	M_2	X_2
Z-goods	Z	X_{31}	X_{32}	0	C_3	I_3	N_3	M_3	X_3
Imports in kind	N	X_{n1}	X_{n2}	X_{n3}	C_n	I_n	0	0	X_n
Imports (monetized)	M	X_{m1}	X_{m2}	X_{m3}	C_m	I_m	0	0	X_m
Labor	H	X_{h1}	X_{h2}	X_{h3}	C_h	0	N_h	M_h	X_h
Land	T	X_{t1}	X_{t2}	X_{t3}	C_t	0	0	0	X_t
Agricultural goods	A	S_{11}	S_{12}	S_{13}					S_1
Animals	P	S_{21}	S_{22}	S_{23}					S_2
Tools	Z	S_{31}	S_{32}	S_{33}					S_3

for blankets and clothes). Part is consumed as meat, milk, eggs and skins; part is invested, as when the stock of animals is increased; and part is exported.

Z-goods constitute a varied list, of which the main elements are the following:

(a) processed food: *chuño, chicha*, cheese and dried meat;
(b) textiles: clothes, blankets, ponchos, sweaters, cloaks, sacks, straps, harnesses and lassos;
(c) tools, and repair thereof;
(d) construction: houses, public buildings, yards and enclosures, roads, canals, and construction materials such as adobe bricks and roof-tiles;
(e) fuel: firewood;
(f) trade;
(g) transport;
(h) other crafts: ceramics, leatherwork, carpentry.

Some of these Z-goods contribute to agricultural and cattle production, others to final demand. They contribute to agriculture as sacks and other containers and in the repair of tools; they contribute to cattle production as ropes, harnesses and lassos; they are consumed as woolen textiles; they are invested in construction; and they are exported as cheese.

Imported products from the rural economy (X_n) go into production as agricultural inputs, as inputs for livestock production (black salt fed to animals) or as inputs for the production of Z-goods. They also are consumed, as in the case of maize imported by upper-highland communities, and invested. The same can be said of urban imports: fertilizers, pesticides, medicines for livestock, and dyes for handicrafts are intermediate production goods; salt, sugar and kerosene are for consumption; and they go to investment (above all as steel implements).

Annual labor, measured in person-days, is used in all three sectors of production, although production may often be in two sectors at once, for example when someone tends cattle and spins wool at the same time. C_h refers to 'consumption of labor', in rest-days or fiestas. N_h and M_h denote exported labor (migrating for temporary work outside the community).

The stock of land (X_t) is measured by area, and is allocated to agricultural production, to livestock production when sown to alfalfa, and to production of Z-goods when used for building. C_t refers to land set aside for homes, plazas or sportsfields.

The last three rows represent *stocks* of capital goods which are used in the current year's production – as opposed to the top three lines which represent *flows*, that is, quantities produced during the year. S_1 represents agricultural stocks required for agricultural production (such as seed, S_{11}). S_2 is the stock of animals used in all three sectors, e.g. for motive power (i.e. oxen), reproduction (expansion of the stock), and transportation. Finally, S_3 represents the stock of tools used in the production of goods in all three sectors.

It should be clear that each column of the table represents the combination of elements of production necessary to produce the corresponding good: it is a vector representing a technological process. The four right-hand columns represent vectors of final demand: the composition of goods consumed, accumulated and exchanged. It will also be noticed that the community produces four types of commodities: agricultural goods, livestock, Z-goods, and labor for export to work temporarily elsewhere in town or country.

An empirical estimate of Table 2.1 would summarize the technological relations, the productive structure and exchange relations in peasant communities. It would also show the specific ways in which the peasant economy is connected to the market economy. This estimate is presented in the next section. Before that, the particular geographical setting of peasant communities must be specified, for the production structure of any community will be influenced by the characteristics of ecological levels under control, micro-climates and so on.

Ecological levels and micro-climates

It is customary to divide Peru into three major regions: coast, sierra and jungle (*selva*). This differentiation is based on the Andean cordillera – the sierra – and coast and jungle are merely the regions situated on either side thereof. But some geographers have proposed alternative divisions. In particular, Pulgar Vidal (1972) insists on the existence of eight ecological 'levels' in Peru. Taking into account the greatest possible number of differentiating factors in the natural environment, Pulgar Vidal distinguishes: coast, *yunga*, *quechua*, *suni*, *puna*, cordillera, upper jungle and lower jungle. In this classification, the region usually known as the sierra is divided into five parts.

The sierra, then, is not homogeneous. It includes a vast range of altitudinal zones, often in close proximity to one another, which comprise numerous types of soil and climate. As pointed out by Julio C. Tello, 'the climatic conditions of the sierra vary from the tropical climates of the valleys and ravines, to the arctic conditions of the high cordillera' (quoted in Pulgar Vidal, p. 13). The clear zonal distinctions made by the inhabitants of the sierra in their immediate environment do in fact correspond to a large extent to the regional classification proposed by Pulgar Vidal.

The five regions mentioned for the sierra define a series of ecological levels. In terms of altitude, the *yunga* ranges up to 2,300 meters and corresponds to the warm valleys; the *quechua*, the temperate region, ranges from 2,300 to 3,500 meters; the *suni* is a cold region ranging from 3,500 to 4,000 meters and the *puna*, the 'treeless zone', rises up to 4,800 meters. Thereafter we reach the cordillera where there is practically no agricultural or pastoral activity of any kind.

Table 2.2 shows the distribution of population among the eight ecological levels in 1972. Although the coast contains 44% of the

Table 2.2 *Peru: total and rural population by ecological region, 1972*

Regions	Altitude (meters)	Total population '000	Total population %	Rural population '000	Rural population %
Coast	Under 500	5,929	43.8	1,208	17.0
Yunga	500–2,000	926	6.9	725	10.2
	(500–1,000)	(228)	(1.7)	(122)	(1.7)
	(1,000–1,500)	(258)	(1.9)	(212)	(3.0)
	(1,500–2,000)	(440)	(3.3)	(391)	(5.5)
Quechua	2,000–3,500	4,073	30.1	3,215	45.3
	(2,000–2,500)	(892)	(6.6)	(625)	(8.8)
	(2,500–3,000)	(1,171)	(8.7)	(1,012)	(14.3)
	(3,000–3,500)	(2,010)	(14.8)	(1,578)	(22.2)
Suni	3,500–4,000	1,325	9.8	1,101	15.5
Puna	4,000–4,500	192	1.4	124	1.7
Cordillera	4,500 and above	13	0.1	9	0.1
High jungle	500–1,000	371	2.7	280	3.9
Low jungle	under 500	709	5.2	444	6.3
		13,538	100.0	7,106	100.0

Note: The estimates were calculated on the basis of district population figures in the *National Population Census of 1972.* However, they remain approximations because the altitude of each district was assumed to be the same as the altitude of the district capital. The altitudes were obtained from the *Anuario Estadístico del Perú*, Vol. 3, Table 2.2.6 (Lima, Oficina Nacional de Estadísticas y Censos, n.d.) and from inquiries at the Instituto Geográfico Militar.

According to Pulgar Vidal the *quechua* begins at 2,300 meters and the cordillera at 4,800. Since the intervals in our sources were 500 meters, a small and insignificant part of the area covered by the *yunga* had to be included in the *quechua*, while the cordillera was defined as starting at 4,500 meters, thus impinging slightly on the *puna*. However, these errors are marginal.

nation's population, 25% live in Lima. The next most important region is the *quechua*, with 30% of the population. Rising from coast to *quechua*, only 7% of the population are to be found in the *yunga* because of its harsh environment and very steep terrain. Above the *quechua* the population again declines until one passes the cordillera and descends the eastern slopes of the Andes to the upper jungle.

Taking the rural population alone – 53% of the nation – the heaviest concentration is found in the *quechua* (45%), followed by the coast (17%), the *suni* (16%) and the *yunga* (10%). Thus the five ecological levels of the sierra comprise 73% of the rural and 39% of the national population.

Each ecological level evidently exhibits different production possibilities. For each zone Pulgar Vidal lists 'limit products' which cannot be produced at higher altitudes. For the *yunga* these are sugar cane and certain varieties of fruit (avocado, *lúcumo*, chirimoya (prickly pear), *guayava* and citrus fruits). As far as the upper limits of the *quechua* one finds maize, wheat, and other fruit (plums, peaches, apples and quinces); and in the case of the *suni* the 'limit products' are beans, small tubers (oca, *olluco, mashua*), high-altitude cereals (*quinua, cañihua*) and vegetables such as *tarhui*. These products of the *suni* also have a lower limit of cultivation at the border of the *suni* and *quechua*. Finally, only potatoes and barley can still be cultivated on the *puna*, and even then only in some places and with lengthy fallow periods. Barley cannot be cultivated lower than the *quechua*, but potatoes grow in all the sierra regions.

The ecological levels are also marked by variations in the possibilities of livestock production. For example, the cameloids (llamas, alpacas and the like) pasture mostly on the *puna*, while equine and caprine animals are most suited to the lower regions. Given the variation in both flora and fauna, the production possibilities of non-agricultural goods (Z-goods) are also influenced heavily by access to ecological levels. Finally, it should be remembered that even within each ecological level a wide variety of micro-climates is to be found and, as a result, individual communities possess a wide variety of resources. On the other hand, these resources differ between communities for they have access to different ecological levels and micro-climates, which implies that communities have different production possibility sets.

The sample

The next chapters will present the results of research carried out in the southern sierra of Peru, the poorest area of the sierra region in income terms. The peasant families studied are minifundistas, possessing for the most part fewer than five hectares of land; and they are organized in peasant *comunidades*. The family (or household) and the *comunidad* are therefore the units of analysis throughout the study.

Eight communities were selected from a sample universe which contained the most important areas with peasant communities in the southern sierra. The communities vary in their ecological characteristics: Jacantaya, Culta and Ninamarca are typical of the *suni* zone; Acobamba of the *yunga*, and the remainder are in the *quechua*. The only one of the five departments in the area which is not represented is Ayacucho, but this is not of importance since differences *between* departments are minor.

The data were obtained by uniform questionnaires administered to peasant families in all the communities. Other informants were also interviewed, in particular persons who occupied or had occupied positions of responsibility in the communities; these provided invaluable information on the social and physical context of the study which shed further light on the information provided by the families interviewed, and also enabled us to detect when the information given by the families was clearly beyond the bounds of local possibilities. The research in these communities was initiated in 1976 with several visits and preliminary data collection (Figueroa, 1978). The final stage in data collection, which was initiated in September 1978, lasted two weeks in each community and was carried out by an average of four persons, three of whom worked in all the localities and one of whom was usually a person from the community itself. In cases where the family concerned possessed a faulty command of Spanish the interviews were conducted in Quechua or Aymara. The data collected on flows refer to the previous year ending before the interview. The fieldwork ended in April 1979.

Table 2.3 shows the distribution of the sample families among the eight communities. It was decided to sample about 40 families in each community, in order to be able to carry out a statistical analysis of the results by communities. All the families interviewed, including replacements, were selected by random sampling. Therefore, each sample is representative of its community. On the basis of population data, weights were applied to the sample of families to make it representative of the eight communities and the southern sierra. The reader will find in each table the average values for these levels of sample expansion as 'sample total' and 'southern sierra' respectively. (For further details on the sample the reader is referred to Appendix I.)

Table 2.3 *The sample communities*

Name	Date of study		Number of families interviewed	Department
Accha-Sihuina (SIH)	Sept.	1978	41	Cuzco
Ninamarca (NIN)	Oct.	1978	31	Cuzco
Acobamba-San Marcos (ACO)	Nov.	1978	40	Huancavelica
Ancobamba (ANC)	Dec.	1978	40	Apurimac
Ttiomayo (TTI)	Jan.	1979	36	Cuzco
Huando (HUA)	Feb.	1979	42	Huancavelica
Culta (CUL)	March	1979	40	Puno
Jacantaya (JAC)	April	1979	36	Puno
Total			306	

3

The economic unit and economic organization

In order to study the functioning of the peasant economy the basic economic unit of such a system must be clearly established. Who has the control of resources? Who makes the decisions on the allocation of these resources? Who makes the decisions on consumption and accumulation? This chapter is devoted to answering such questions.

Size of family and labor force

In this study, the family is defined as all those persons who habitually live in the same house. The criterion of residence poses some difficulties on account of permanent and temporary migration, and the rule adopted was to consider as resident any person who lived in the house a total of six months or more in the preceding year.

The average family size varies between 4.2 and five members in the communities (Table 3.1). The variation in these average sizes seems to bear no particular relation to the community's ecological level. Although the value of the standard deviation between family size within each community is high, the differences between communities seem to be small. These data show that it is difficult to identify a 'typical' peasant family size, at least without taking into account the stage of the household cycle reached by each one.

This study uses two definitions of labor force. The first, designed to take into account the role of children in production, and thus to show the family's productive capacity, includes all members of six years or more of age. The second includes persons of 18 years or more of age and measures the 'adult labor force'. Starting from 18 years of age, people can carry out adult tasks and they can also obtain identity cards which enable them to move about more easily in the labor market. Neither definition excludes elderly people since there is no formal 'retirement age' – like the children, they too participate in

13

Table 3.1 *Size of family and labor force (number of persons)*

Community	Size of family		Labor force			
			Total		Adult	
	$\bar{X}$	S	$\bar{X}$	S	$\bar{X}$	S
Jacantaya	4.6	(2.6)	3.9	(2.2)	2.6	(1.3)
Culta	4.5	(2.0)	3.6	(1.7)	2.2	(0.7)
Ninamarca	4.7	(1.4)	3.6	(1.3)	2.2	(0.5)
Ancobamba	4.7	(2.5)	3.7	(1.7)	2.1	(0.7)
Ttiomayo	5.0	(2.2)	3.9	(1.6)	2.3	(0.9)
Sihuina	4.3	(1.9)	3.6	(1.5)	2.3	(0.8)
Huando	4.8	(2.6)	3.7	(1.8)	2.1	(0.8)
Acobamba	4.2	(1.7)	3.4	(1.4)	2.1	(0.6)
Sample total	4.6		3.7		2.2	
Southern sierra	4.5		3.6		2.2	

Note: $\bar{X}$ = average; S = standard deviation.

production. Table 3.1 also shows that, under the first definition, 'total labor force' varies between 3.4 and 3.9 persons per family, while 'adult labor force' varies between 2.1 and 2.6. Once again, there is a wide dispersion in the measure of total labor force, but this dispersion is reduced for the measure of adult labor force: the vast majority of the families have between two and three adult members, and in this respect one can speak of a typical peasant family.

A further, equally important, observation is that the peasant family is typically a nuclear family. It is extremely rare to find a household with more than one married couple, and even in Culta, where 20% of the households had four or more adult members, only a very small proportion of these included two married couples. Hence, the concepts of 'family' and 'household' coincide in the peasant communities and can be used interchangeably.

Land: uses, tenure and fragmentation

In the peasant communities two types of land may be distinguished: cultivable and natural pasture. Whereas pasture land can be used for only one purpose (livestock production), cultivable land can have alternative uses: it can be planted to crops, it can be used to cultivate pastures, or it can be left uncultivated. If it is uncultivated it can still serve as natural pasture. In this sense, uncultivated land does not imply idle land; it means that land leaves the agricultural process and enters into livestock production.

Pasture land is always communal property and is collectively utilized. Each family has free access to it and derives economic benefit in proportion to the family's holding of livestock. The tenure system of arable land varies from community to community; in some there is overall private ownership, and each family uses the land according to its own interest; whereas in others, part of the arable land is used under a system of collective rotation. This is the case for the low quality, marginal land that must be left uncultivated after two to three years of cultivation. If the families' individual plots are not protected with fences, the areas for cultivation *must* be decided collectively so as to keep animals off that area. The utilization of marginal lands for crop and livestock production requires a collective rotation of land. The land where rotation is done collectively is called *laymi* and is divided into several areas for the annual rotation.[1] Needless to say, once the area of cultivation is decided, the decision as to what to produce and how to produce is made by each family individually.

Table 3.2 shows the distribution of arable land between pasture and crops. The unit of measurement is the number of plots rather than hectares because of the imprecision of replies to questions concerning the size of plots; moreover, the enormous number of plots belonging to each family made the estimation of their aggregate size impossible. Estimation in terms of number of plots is an adequate approximation because the use of the plots is independent of their size. The proportion of land assigned to agriculture, rather than pasture, varies among the communities between 46% and 90%.

In six of the eight communities there exists the *laymi* system. Jacantaya does not possess this system because it is located on the shores of Lake Titicaca and its land is cultivated in terraces. The terraces are small and possess clear boundaries, so that a family can leave a plot fallow and use it for pasture even while the neighboring parcel is being cultivated. The other community which does not have a *laymi* system is Huando. This community did have such a system until some 20 years ago, and its disappearance is mainly due to the introduction of modern inputs, mainly fertilizers, which have raised the productivity of the land. Table 3.2 shows the importance of the *laymi* system in the other communities: between 21% and 71% of the

Table 3.2 *Distribution of cultivable parcels between cultivated and fallow land (number of parcels per family)*

Community	Type of tenure	Cultivated	Fallow	Total
Jacantaya	Private	19.5	15.1	34.6
Culta	Private	11.3	0.6	11.9
	Laymi	27.6	44.9	72.5
	Total	38.9	45.5	84.4
Ninamarca	Private	2.3	1.4	3.7
	Laymi	4.7	3.8	8.5
	Total	7.0	5.2	12.2
Ancobamba	Private	6.5	0.9	7.4
	Laymi	1.8	n.a.	n.a.
	Total	8.3	n.a.	n.a.
Ttiomayo	Private	2.9	0	2.9
	Laymi	3.1	2.7	5.8
	Total	6.0	2.7	8.7
Huando	Private	8.5	1.0	9.5
Acobamba	Private	2.5	0.3	2.8
	Laymi	1.6	4.1	5.7
	Total	4.1	4.4	8.5

Note: Data for Sihuina were not available.

land cultivated during the years of our research was under this system. Its qualitative importance is further underlined by the observation that it was in these lands that basic food products such as potatoes were cultivated.

Table 3.2 also shows the extreme degree of fragmentation of cultivable holdings, the number of holdings per family ranging from nine to 84. In the extreme cases of Culta and Jacantaya parcels are measured in furrows, which are at most 20 meters long. One frequently hears a peasant saying that he has 'one plot of four furrows, another of six furrows' and so on. A family's plots are generally distributed across the different ecological levels to which the community has access; however, there are often several plots even within a given ecological level belonging to the same family.

This fragmentation can be explained in part by the desire of producers to avoid erosion, when the land is sloped. But the existence of fragmentation on flat land shows that there are also demographic and economic factors involved. Families acquire land upon their formation via inter-generational transfer, and these new families must also gain access to land on different ecological levels if they are to produce a range of products. The need of a 'vertical control of ecology' by each family implies a process of land fragmentation in the inter-generational transfer. Although this need would seem to reflect a strategy aiming at a certain degree of family self-sufficiency, such a hypothesis does not take into account the wide variations in micro-climates, even within the same ecological level, which create variations in yields as a result of frost, hail and floods. Thus the spread of parcels would seem to reflect also a form of risk-averse economic behavior, which would certainly be consistent with the low level of the producers' incomes.

The number of crops sown and parcels cultivated by each family is shown in Table 3.3. The crops involved are: potatoes, barley, *oca*, *olluco*, *mashua*, *quinoa*, *cañihua*, *tarhui*, broad beans, wheat, peas and kidney beans. The average number of parcels cultivated per family varies between communities from four to 39, and in all the communities there are more parcels than crops, implying that families grow one crop in more than one parcel. Thus in Jacantaya eight crops are sown on an average of 20 parcels. Only in Acobamba is there near-equality between the average number of parcels and the average number of crops. The diversification of crop-location is even greater than this indicates, since there is much inter-cropping. This offers further support to the risk-aversion hypothesis.

Capital goods

The capital stock of the peasant economy consists of three types of goods which are used in the production process: agricultural goods (mainly seed), animals and tools. Seed is generally obtained from the same crops; they are rarely bought by the peasant families. Consistent with its portfolio of crops, each family must hold a portfolio of seeds. The stock of seed per family was not estimated but it clearly varies with the amount of cultivated land.

Animals can be divided into three types, depending on their place

Table 3.3 *Number of parcels cultivated by number of crops (% of families)*

Number of crops	Communities						
	JAC	CUL	NIN	ANC	TTI	HUA	ACO
0						7.1	2.6
1				5.0		0	0
2			3.2	0		2.4	7.7
3			9.7	2.5	27.8	2.4	28.2
4	2.4	5.1	9.7	10.0	36.1	7.1	25.6
5	2.8	7.7	19.4	7.5	19.4	11.9	20.5
6	13.9	12.8	29.0	22.5	11.1	26.2	2.6
7	22.2	17.9	19.4	12.5	5.6	16.7	7.7
8	16.7	20.5	9.7	20.0		19.0	2.6
9	11.1	20.5		15.0		2.4	0
10	13.9	10.3		2.5		2.4	2.6
11	13.9	5.1		0		2.4	
12	2.8			2.5			
Total (%)	100.0	100.0	100.0	100.0	100.0	100.0	100.0
Number of crops							
Average	8.2	7.7	5.6	6.6	4.3	6.0	4.2
Standard dev.	2.0	1.8	1.6	2.3	1.2	2.4	1.8
Number of parcels							
Average	19.5	38.9	7.1	8.2	6.1	8.5	4.1
Standard dev.	18.3	19.3	2.7	3.5	2.4	5.0	2.0

Note: Data for Sihuina were not available.

in the production process. One type is used for consumption of its products, in the form of meat, wool, milk and eggs. This includes sheep, alpaca, pigs, goats, and minor domestic animals such as chickens and guinea-pigs. The second type of animal is used in productive services, such as horses, donkeys, mules and llamas. Cattle are considered the third type for they provide both consumption and productive services. Each family's mix of these types will obviously influence the overall structure of its activities.

It will be seen from Table 3.4 that, on average, the peasant family has very few animals: the typical family possesses 7 sheep, 1 pig, 3 chickens, 4 guinea-pigs and 2 head of cattle. (These figures appear as weighted averages in the last column of the table.) However, the composition of the stock varies substantially between communities, largely on account of ecological differences. Goats are not found in the higher communities, nor are llamas or alpacas found in the lower ones. But there remain other differences even in those animals which can be kept at all these altitudes, and these have an economic explanation. The communities with most cattle and sheep are Ancobamba, Culta, Ttiomayo and Ninamarca, and those with the least are Huando and Acobamba. In Acobamba the land slopes steeply, and there is thus the constant risk of falls, while in Huando there is an ecological explanation as well as an economic one: the community has no high pasture lands, and therefore does not control enough ecological levels to practice both agriculture and cattle-raising at the same time.

Variation in the endowment of horses is largely explained by distance from a road. Ancobamba and Sihuina are the communities furthest from the road in the sample and they have the higher average of horses per family. The use of oxen in ploughing is limited when deeper ploughing, beyond their capacity, is required, and when land

Table 3.4 *Animal stocks: number of animals per family*

Animals	JAC	CUL	NIN	ANC	TTI	SIH	HUA	ACO	Sample total
Sheep	6.39	13.08	12.32	4.85	6.97	5.56	3.74	4.03	6.95
Pigs	0.44	1.74	2.42	1.35	1.92	0.61	0.71	0.67	1.09
Goats	0.00	0.00	0.00	1.85	0.00	0.10	0.91	0.15	
Alpaca	0.00	2.67	0.00	0.00	0.00	0.00	0.00	0.00	
Chickens	1.64	2.92	1.94	1.78	2.67	2.93	2.17	3.85	2.51
Guinea-pigs	0.89	0.59	5.45	5.95	8.62	4.22	2.95	3.36	3.94
Horses	0.14	1.40	1.13	2.68	0.45	1.71	1.05	0.63	1.17
Llamas	0.00	0.05	0.05	0.00	0.00	0.00	0.00	0.00	
Oxen	0.14	0.75	0.94	0.53	1.03	0.54	0.57	0.10	0.56
Total cattle	1.33	2.08	3.03	3.65	3.47	2.39	1.00	1.59	2.29

is too steep or is cultivated in terraces. It is for these latter reasons that there are few oxen in Jacantaya and Acobamba. But in general, it can be seen that animal draught power is limited, and that to a significant degree the peasant economy depends on human energy. This brings us to its implements. These are of two types: those used in agriculture, such as oxploughs, foot-ploughs (*chakitajlla*), hoes and spades; and those used in the production of non-agricultural goods (Z-goods), especially in construction, such as picks and shovels, and sewing-machines.

Table 3.5 shows that the typical peasant family uses a very small range of tools requiring human energy: between 1 and 2 foot-ploughs, 3 hoes and 2 picks. The variation in the number of foot-ploughs per family as between different communities is largely explained by differences in the quality of land: in Jacantaya oxen cannot be used because of terrace cultivation, and in Ancobamba the poor quality of the soil requires deeper ploughing than can be obtained with oxen. The variations in hoes and spades seem to be related to differences between families of varying wealth, while sewing-machines are a preliminary indication of the wealth of a community, and above all of its modernization. Huando thus appears as the most modern of these communities, followed by the two communities in the department of Puno: Culta and Jacantaya.

The economic unit and economic organization in peasant communities

The exposition hitherto has shown that, typically, the peasant of the southern sierra family has an adult labor force of about two persons;

Table 3.5 *Stocks of implements per family*

Implements	Communities								Sample total
	JAC	CUL	NIN	ANC	TTI	SIH	HUA	ACO	
Foot-ploughs	2.71	0.87	1.13	1.90	1.14	1.56	1.95	1.53	1.57
Hoes	2.83	4.08	1.71	2.63	1.94	2.44	3.71	3.85	3.12
Sewing-machines	0.31	0.41	0.14	0.08	0.17	0.12	0.55	0.10	0.28
Picks and shovels	2.29	2.39	2.19	2.19	3.06	1.86	1.44	3.22	2.40

two or three hectares of cultivable land divided into a number of parcels (between nine and 84) and access to a variable amount of pasture land under collective use; its animal stock consists of 2 head of cattle, 7 sheep, 1 pig, 1 horse, 2 or 3 chickens and 4 guinea-pigs; its stock of tools consists of 1 foot-plough, 3 hoes and 2 picks. The family's resource endowment is used in agricultural and livestock production and in the production of non-agricultural goods and services (Z-goods). In addition to the self-employment of its resources, the family exchanges part of them particularly family labor.

Apart from the adult labor force, resource endowment per family varies significantly between communities, especially in the case of land. The land endowment depends on the community's access to different ecological levels and on the topography of its land. Ecological characteristics define production possibilities, and topography is an important determinant of the technology in use.

In terms of control of resources it has been shown that individual families own and control the arable land and the capital goods in the peasant communities. Pastures are collectively owned and used but animals belong to individual families. On the other hand, the allocation of resources is also decided by individual families. The allocation of the family labor to agriculture, livestock production, Z-goods and labor exchange is a family decision. What to produce, in which plots and with what mix of inputs are also family decisions. Moreover, the risk, gains and losses in production are assumed by the individual family. In terms of control of resources, capacity to decide on the allocation of those resources to alternative uses, and appropriation of the net output produced, the unit of production is, clearly, the peasant family.

Nevertheless, the peasant family does not operate in isolation from the rest of the community. In the productive process the family establishes relations with the rest of the families of the community. When a family has an excess demand or supply of a good or of labor (which is frequent), there are up to three possible ways of achieving equilibrium: reciprocity, barter and monetary exchange. Reciprocity is a form of exchange in which the lending of a service is paid back with the same service in a not very distant time period. It is a special form of loan, without interest. If three days of labor are received, three days of labor are returned; if two days' use of an ox are received, the same amount of services must be returned. It is clear that this exchange has a technological justification, since with this reciprocity it is possible to obtain optimum factor proportions in production.

The most common form of exchange by reciprocity is the exchange of labor. Family labor may not be sufficient to put a roof on a house, or to carry out the labors of planting or harvesting. This system, referred to as *ayni* or *minka*, adopts in many cases festive forms where goods (determined culturally) are consumed. In this case production and consumption are inseparable in the production process, and the criterion of efficiency, that is, of producing at the minimum economic cost, is not applicable. The criterion of efficiency establishes, it appears, the lower limit to the factor proportions required technologically in an activity.

The existence of barter, that is, the exchange of a good or service for another good or service, indicates that the excess demands and supplies of the families are of different magnitudes. The case of reciprocity is given when these quantities are of the same magnitude; thus in a community with few differences in the ownership of resources, reciprocity would dominate. Many families derive income from the exchange of the services of their work animals, tools, land and labor. To this we would have to add credit. These productive services are paid in different ways, sometimes with food or non-food goods, sometimes with other types of productive services. Finally, there is exchange of productive services for money. This form of exchange clearly becomes necessary given the limitations of bartering, that is to say, its dependence on the complementarity between two parties' supply and demand of goods and services. In all of the communities studied there exists a market for productive services, with transparent monetary prices.

Once it has been shown that the family is the unit of production in the peasant communities, it will be much easier to show that the family is also the unit of consumption. In fact, the basket of consumption of goods and services is determined by the family. The actions taken to acquire that basket, i.e. consumption of own-production or exchange, are also family decisions. The fact that capital goods are owned by individual families is sufficient to show that capital accumulation is a family decision too. Thus the family is the unit of production and consumption – that is, the economic unit – in the peasant communities.

However, not everything is under the control and decision of individual families in the peasant communities. Some resources are subject to collective control – the case of pasture land has already been mentioned. This case also includes the use of natural pastures grown in the rotated land (*laymi*) when it is in the fallow period. In some communities, even the stubble in the arable land of individual families is open to all the community as collective pastures. Water is another resource which is under collective control and is managed through collective decisions.

As far as land resources are concerned, only in Ninamarca and Sihuina was found communal arable land. In Ninamarca there exists a plot of land which is cultivated collectively; the net income it generates is used to finance the construction of public buildings (like schools) or other public works. In Sihuina the communal land is given mainly to families in charge of the communal fiesta in order to help them with the expenses of such celebrations. There were no communal lands that were used to distribute to new families.[2]

The peasant community also imposes some economic obligations on individual families. One of these is the labor time that every family must supply for public works. It is through this system that a community can increase and maintain its social infrastructure (roads, canals, buildings). In economic terms, this is equivalent to a local tax system that is collected in labor time levied equally upon everyone. In the eight communities studied the number of man-days per year that a family had to supply to the community was between four and 20.

The existence of resources under collective control and decision sets some limits to the economic decisions of the individual family. However, those constraints do not imply that the peasant family could not be the economic unit; they do imply that these units operate within particular economic and institutional frameworks. To elucidate the particular circumstances in which the peasant economy operates in Peru today will be the object of the following chapters. Thus, the next chapter explores the quantitative aspects of the production and exchange processes in peasant communities.

4

Production and exchange

Intersectoral flows

Table 4.1 shows the intersectoral flows in six of the eight communities studied; that is, it replaces the symbols of Table 2.1 with empirical data, with one modification: the production of each separate sector of intermediate goods – the first three columns of Table 2.1 – has been consolidated into one column. This has been done for the sake of simplicity and also because it is often difficult to separate the production of intermediate goods by sector. The N column refers to non-monetary barter transactions, and the M column to monetary transactions. The former principally measures transactions with other communities, the latter transactions with the rest of the economy, above all the urban economy. Two of the communities – Ttiomayo and Sihuina – have been omitted on account of the incompleteness of the data, but the other six are sufficiently well distributed among ecological levels for the representativeness of the sample not to be affected significantly. Of course, whenever only these six communities have been used in tabulations, the weights of the sampled families have been changed accordingly to get the expanded values for 'sample total' and 'southern sierra'.

The reader will note that Table 4.1 contains certain identities. The figure at the bottom of column 1 is the same as the $A + P + Z$ in the last column. The former represents the value of production viewed from the side of the cost of production whereas the latter is the value of production by destination (deliveries), and both must be equal. Because of this identity, self-employment (row 20) was estimated by difference. The transactions in kind have been transformed into monetary values by applying average market prices observed in the monetary transactions. Obviously, the valuation of imports to the community must be equal to the valuation of exports when exchange

Table 4.1 *Intersectoral relations in peasant communities (soles per year, per family)*

		$A+P+Z$ Inter-mediate goods (1)	C Consump-tion (2)	I Invest-ment (3)	N Exports in kind (4)	M Exports monetized (5)	Total (6)
					Jacantaya		
A	(Agriculture) (1)	3,700	14,896	0	2,854	5,401	26,851
P_1	(Derived products) (2)	990	1,680	0	0	107	2,777
P_2	(Consumption) (3)	0	1,151	0	7	325	1,483
P_3	(Services) (4)	0	0	0	0	0	0
P_4	(Cattle) (5)	0	594	0	0	5,603	6,197
P_5	(Other) (6)	0	0	0	0	0	0
P	(Livestock) (7)	990	3,425	0	7	6,035	10,457
Z_1	(Manuf.) (8)	0	3,825	0	0	482	4,307
Z_2	(Trade) (9)	0	0	0	0	3,213	3,213
Z_3	(Other) (10)	0	5,685	0	0	9,682	15,367
Z	(Z-goods) (11)	0	9,510	0	0	13,377	22,887
$A+P+Z$	(12)	4,690	27,831	0	2,861	24,813	60,195
N	(Imports in kind) (13)	1,000	1,861	0			2,861
M	(Imports in money) (14)	4,836	36,638	2,584			44,058
$N+M+A+P+Z$	(15)	10,526	66,330	2,584			

Table 4.1 (*cont.*)

| | | | Jacantaya | | | | |
		A+P+Z (1)	C (2)	I (3)	N (4)	M (5)	Total (6)
Wages – N	(16)	41			0	0	0
Wages – M	(17)	4,644			0	12,772	
Rents – N	(18)	0					
Rents – M	(19)	72					
Self-employment	(20)	44,912					
Total		60,195			2,861	37,585	25,548
Net transfer	(21)				0	6,473	
				Culta			
A (Agriculture)	(1)	4,966	19,866	0	287	429	25,548
P_1 (Derived products)	(2)	2,145	3,066	0	0	1,502	6,713
P_2 (Consumption)	(3)	0	3,291	0	0	2,541	5,832
P_3 (Services)	(4)	0	0	0	0	316	316
P_4 (Cattle)	(5)	0	594	0	25	20,100	20,719
P_5 (Other)	(6)	0	0	0	0	408	408
P (Livestock)	(7)	2,145	6,951	0	25	24,867	33,988
Z_1 (Manuf.)	(8)	0	4,358	0	0	0	4,358
Z_2 (Trade)	(9)	0	0	0	0	3,357	3,357

						Total
Z_3 (Other) (10)	0	0	0		1,715	1,715
Z (Z-goods) (11)	0	4,358	0		5,072	9,430
$A+P+Z$ (12)	7,111	31,175	0	312	30,368	68,966
N (Imports in kind) (13)	44	243	25			312
M (Imports in money) (14)	2,707	33,812	4,867			41,386
$N+M+A+P+Z$ (15)	9,862	65,230	4,892			
Wages − N (16)		1,000	0		0	
Wages − M (17)		2,052	0		9,403	
Rents − N (18)		19				
Rents − M (19)		298				
Self-employment (20)	312	55,735				
Total		68,966		312	39,771	
Net transfer (21)					1,615	

Ninamarca

						Total
A (Agriculture) (1)	2,345	9,380	837		12,685	25,247
P_1 (Derived products) (2)	1,980	2,100	13		0	4,093
P_2 (Consumption) (3)	0	9,644	77		2,594	12,315
P_3 (Services) (4)	0	0	0		0	0
P_4 (Cattle) (5)	0	2,560	742		3,000	6,302
P_5 (Other) (6)	0	0	0		680	680
P (Livestock) (7)	1,980	14,304	832		6,274	23,390
Z_1 (Manuf.) (8)	0	2,900	116		448	3,464
Z_2 (Trade) (9)	0	0	0		1,232	1,232

Table 4.1 (cont.)

		Ninamarca					
		$A+P+Z$ (1)	C (2)	I (3)	N (4)	M (5)	Total (6)
Z_3 (Other)	(10)	0	0	0	0	32	32
Z (Z-goods)	(11)	0	2,900	0	116	1,712	4,728
$A+P+Z$	(12)	4,325	26,584	0	1,785	20,671	53,365
N (Imports in kind)	(13)	125	601	1,059			1,785
M (Imports in money)	(14)	1,755	17,597	1,461			20,813
$N+M+A+P+Z$	(15)	6,205	44,782	2,520			
Wages – N	(16)	137			0	0	
Wages – M	(17)	908			0	142	
Rents – N	(18)	0					
Rents – M	(19)	0					
Self-employment	(20)	46,115					
Total		53,365			1,785	20,813	
Net transfer	(21)					0	

A (Agriculture)	(1)	8,777	35,046		351	356	44,530
P_1 (Derived products)	(2)	825	1,869		0	0	2,694
P_2 (Consumption)	(3)	0	2,202		98	186	2,486
P_3 (Services)	(4)	0	0		0	925	925
P_4 (Cattle)	(5)	0	863		0	5,324	6,187
P_5 (Other)	(6)	0	0		5	360	365
P (Livestock)	(7)	825	4,934		103	6,795	12,657
Z_1 (Manuf.)	(8)	0	531		5	209	745
Z_2 (Trade)	(9)	0	0		0	1,843	1,843
Z_3 (Other)	(10)	0	0		5	84	89
Z (Z-goods)	(11)	0	531		10	2,136	2,677
$A+P+Z$	(12)	9,602	40,511	0	464	9,287	59,864
N (Imports in kind)	(13)	188	63	213			464
M (Imports in money)	(14)	1,038	17,619	910			19,567
$N+M+A+P+Z$	(15)	10,828	58,193	1,123			
Wages $-N$	(16)	60			0	0	
Wages $-M$	(17)	1,162			0	8,458	
Rents $-N$	(18)	60					
Rents $-M$	(19)	17					
Self-employment	(20)	47,737					
Total	(21)	59,864			464	17,745	
Net transfer						1,822	

Huando

A (Agriculture)	(1)	7,821	32,210	0	134	10,050	50,215
P_1 (Derived products)	(2)	2,000	3,000	0	0	293	5,293

Table 4.1 (cont.)

	Huando					
	$A+P+Z$ (1)	C (2)	I (3)	N (4)	M (5)	Total (6)
P_2 (Consumption) (3)	0	2,710	0	73	2,898	5,681
P_3 (Services) (4)	0	0	0	0	352	352
P_4 (Cattle) (5)	0	1,000	0	0	3,642	4,642
P_5 (Other) (6)	0	0	0	0	0	0
P (Livestock) (7)	2,000	6,710	0	73	7,185	15,968
Z_1 (Manuf.) (8)	0	0	0	0	0	0
Z_2 (Trade) (9)	0	0	0	21	15,646	15,667
Z_3 (Other) (10)	0	0	0	0	9,083	9,083
Z (Z-goods) (11)	0	0	0	21	24,729	24,750
$A+P+Z$ (12)	9,821	38,920	0	228	41,964	90,933
N (Imports in kind) (13)	0	201	27	—	—	228
M (Imports in money) (14)	4,114	46,421	2,536	—	—	53,071
$N+M+A+P+Z$ (15)	13,935	85,542	2,563			
Wages $- N$ (16)	177			0		
Wages $- M$ (17)	8,506			—	4,520	
Rents $- N$ (18)	1,122			—		

Acobamba

							Total
A	(Agriculture)	(1)	6,222	24,888	0	362	4,557	36,029
P_1	(Derived products)	(2)	2,000	6,000	0	0	0	8,000
P_2	(Consumption)	(3)	0	2,240	0	161	1,048	3,449
P_3	(Services)	(4)	0	0	0	0	0	0
P_4	(Cattle)	(5)	0	1,000	0	0	1,538	2,538
P_5	(Other)	(6)	0	0	0	0	92	92
P	(Livestock)	(7)	2,000	9,240	0	161	2,678	14,079
Z_1	(Manuf.)	(8)	0	117	0	0	5	122
Z_2	(Trade)	(9)	0	0	0	0	15,282	15,282
Z_3	(Other)	(10)	0	0	0	0	410	410
Z	(Z-goods)	(11)	0	117	0	0	15,697	15,814
$A+P+Z$		(12)	8,222	34,245	0	523	22,932	65,922
N	(Imports in kind)	(13)	400	105	18	0		523
M	(Imports in money)	(14)	1,138	24,868	1,331			27,337
$N+M+A+P+Z$		(15)	9,760	59,218	1,349			
Wages $- N$		(16)	715			0	0	
Wages $- M$		(17)	10,335			0	3,841	
Rents $- N$		(18)	425					
Rents $- M$		(19)	0					
Self-employment		(20)	44,687					
Total			65,922			523	26,773	
Net transfer		(21)	0			0	564	

is in kind. This explains the equality between the value at the bottom of column 4 and at the end of row 13. For the monetary exchange the difference of total value of exports and total value of imports is due to net transfers that families in the community receive from relatives living in the city. Therefore, the last two figures at the bottom of column 5 must be equal to the figure at the end of row 14.

The entries in Table 4.1 are all monetary values: *soles* per year, per family. Therefore, the values for all communities are comparable since differences in population have been eliminated. To be sure, the total annual values for a community can be found by multiplying the entries in Table 4.1 by the number of families in the community shown in Table 2.3, and hence Table 4.1 shows the production and exchange structure of the communities.

Intermediate goods

There are three types of intermediate good (defined according to source) in the communities: domestic goods, derived from each family's own production; goods imported from other communities; and goods imported from the rest of the economy. Table 4.1 shows that between 45% and 90% of intermediate goods are produced by the families themselves, and almost all the remainder are imported from the urban economy. Within the category of domestically produced intermediate goods, agricultural goods figure most prominently, and among them the principal item is animal feed. The main intermediate product derived from animals is sheep's wool, while the Z sector produces very few intermediate goods. The production of animal feed by the agricultural sector, and of wool for textiles by the animal sector constitute the main technological relationships between the three sectors A, P and Z.

Intermediate goods imported from other communities are few. The table provides estimates for a monetary value for wool, salt, wood, straw and pasture. Wood and straw are used mostly for the construction of houses, and there are a few cases of families renting pasture or stubble for animal feed in neighboring communities. Salt is also fed to animals.

Tables 4.1 and 4.2 show that intermediate goods imported from urban economy consist almost entirely of agricultural inputs: fertilizer and pesticides.[1] Table 4.2 also shows that there are wide variations in the communities' use of modern inputs. Leaving aside

Table 4.2 *Average annual expenditure on modern inputs (soles per year per family)*

Community	Fertilizer	Pesticides	Seed	Animal vaccine	Total
JAC	930 (75)[a]	622 (64)	546 (42)	57 (81)	2,155
CUL	601 (51)	505 (58)	839 (53)	90 (90)	2,035
NIN	404 (23)	832 (93)	358	40 (13)	1,634
ANC	0 (0)	30 (2)	119 (15)	40 (7)	189
TTI	184 (14)	0 (0)	124	6 (10)	314
SIH	15 (2)	81 (34)	179	9 (15)	284
HUA	2,440 (54)	946 (28)	161 (17)	73 (15)	3,620
ACO	364 (8)	154 (5)	475 (23)	8 (15)	1,001

[a] Figures in parentheses = percentage of families purchasing modern inputs.

seeds (which are hardly ever improved varieties) and vaccine for animals (which are an insignificant item in terms of cost), we see that communities such as Ancobamba, Ttiomayo and Sihuina hardly use any fertilizer or pesticides at all. Even in those communities where expenditure on these is relatively high, such as Jacantaya, Culta and Huando – which, as we shall see, are the least poor of all the communities sampled – this is accounted for by a small number of families within them. Of course, the expenditure data do not take into account deficiencies in the method of application of these inputs, which is carried out without any technical assistance. These quantitative and qualitative indications, when combined with the data on capital stocks presented earlier, illustrate the overwhelmingly traditional character of the technology employed in all the communities.

Final demand

The production of the *A*, *P* and *Z* sectors goes to consumption ('own-consumption') and export, since accumulation is almost non-existent (Table 4.1, column 3). In no case does investment exceed 8% of final demand, and it goes as low as 2%, with an overall total of 4%. Clearly, these communities constitute stagnant economies. They are unable to generate any investment from their own resources, and what little investment they do carry out is done with imported goods (column 3, lines 13 and 14). The main capital goods imported are cattle, sheep, chickens and tools. The peasant economy does not appear to have sufficient productive capacity to generate its own surplus in livestock, and although the interviews contained no direct question concerning changes in the family's stock of animals, it was generally agreed that the community's stock was not increasing. On the contrary, it appeared to be declining, due to disease, accidents and thefts. Purchases of livestock, therefore, appear to be merely a replacement of stock rather than its increase. Tools are imported largely because there is no domestic industry for the production of these capital goods. In some cases one finds small workshops in local towns which both carry out repairs and 'manufacture' tools with discarded iron from the cities.

Exports are mainly monetary transactions, and only a small fraction is accounted for by transactions with other communities (columns 4 and 5). The distribution of production between own-consumption and export is almost half-and-half, except in Ancobamba, which is the furthest from a road and where own-consumption is four times as large as exports. Goods exported are exchanged for intermediate goods, for consumer goods and for capital goods (lines 13 and 14).

Own-consumption (column 2, line 12) derives mostly from agricultural goods, followed by animal and their derivatives, with only a small proportion provided by *Z*-goods. The table also shows that a higher proportion of agricultural production goes to own-consumption than from animal or *Z*-good production. Agricultural production is, indeed, mainly for own-consumption; the same can be said of animal derivatives (milk and eggs), sheep and pigs, domestic animals such as guinea-pigs and chickens, and, among *Z*-goods, woolens and other clothes.

The two activities which are clearly undertaken for the purpose of export are cattle-rearing and trade. Cattle are a luxury good at these income levels, and peasant producers prefer to sell their cattle and use the money to buy other consumer goods, rather than consume them directly. The rare occasions when they are consumed arise through commitments imposed at the time of community fiestas.

Trade (line 9) is mainly carried out between the community and the outside, which is why trade is mainly connected with imports and exports. In fact, it is best interpreted as an export of services, selling produce such as cattle outside and bringing products from the cities or from nearby communities. This last is carried out mainly by people attending the weekly markets in a community, including both traders who take community production to the cities and peasants from neighboring communities. Of the eight communities studied, only Sihuina, Huando and Acobamba have weekly markets of their own.

The external sector: monetized exchange

The analysis of monetized imports and exports can draw on data for all eight communities, since data on this subject were collected in the communities excluded from Table 4.1. Table 4.3 shows the structure of exports, with trade presented separately from Z-goods, so that exports of goods are distinguished from exports of services;

Table 4.3 *Structure of monetary exports (%)*

Community	Agri- cultural goods	Live- stock	Z-goods	Trade	Labor	Total
JAC	14.3	16.1	27.1	8.5	34.0	100.0
CUL	1.1	62.5	4.3	8.4	23.7	100.0
NIN	60.9	30.1	2.1	6.1	0.8	100.0
ANC	2.0	38.3	1.6	10.4	47.7	100.0
TTI	33.0	27.4	0.4	0	39.2	100.0
SIH	11.4	27.7	21.0	32.3	7.6	100.0
HUA	21.6	15.5	19.5	33.7	9.7	100.0
ACO	17.0	10.0	0.1	58.6	14.3	100.0
Sample total	13.5	29.2	37.4		19.9	100.0
Southern sierra	14.5	25.2	41.1		19.2	100.0

moreover, income from temporary migrations is added, as exports of labor.

Exports

The first point to emerge from Table 4.3 is the diversified character of the communities' exports: in no community does one item account for more than 63% of total export income, and in four of them one item accounts for 50% or more: cattle in Culta (63%), agricultural products in Ninamarca (61%), trade in Acobamba (59%) and temporary migration in Ancobamba (48%). In three of the communities, 80% of export income is accounted for by two items, in four of them by three items, and in one of them by four items. Given that each item itself constitutes a range of products, the diversified character of their exports becomes evident.

Exports vary widely both within and between communities. If one looks at those sources which account for 33% or more of each community's exports, one finds that agriculture is important in Ninamarca and Ttiomayo, livestock in Culta and Ancobamba, and temporary migration in Jacantaya, Ancobamba and Ttiomayo. Only Z-goods do not reach this proportion in any community, although they account for 27% in Jacantaya, 21% in Sihuina and 20% in Huando.

The specific features of exports vary from community to community. Jacantaya exports almost all the goods and services which are included in the study. In agriculture, due to a favorable micro-climate, it exports mostly green vegetables which are sold at market in a nearby town (Huancane) and are also exchanged directly with neighboring *puna* communities. Income from animal exports consists mainly of cattle. Z-goods exported are mostly fish (mainly the *hispi*) from Lake Titicaca sold in Huancane. Trading income is also derived from dealing in green vegetables.

In Culta, where agriculture is mostly for own-consumption, the main exports are animals, above all cattle. Apart from raising their own, many families buy cattle for fattening and sell them after a few months, financing this activity with their own funds and with loans from the Banco Agrario, which usually amount to about 20,000 *soles*. The most common pattern is for people to buy bulls in September and October and to sell them in April or May. In this way, they take advantage of the time when pasture is most abundant and also use the bulls for ploughing, since at the same time the land is being prepared for sowing. The bank loans are generally for a year. The use and resale activity generates a substantial revenue; this enables the peasant to repay the loan and earn a considerable income. Trading income in this community is also derived from cattle, and the income from fattening was divided equally between trade (Z_2) and income from animals (P_4).

Ninamarca exports a range of products: potatoes, barley for consumption, barley for beer, and oats. Sales of barley to the beer factory in Cuzco, or to intermediaries who then sell to the factory, are slightly more important than other exported products. Animal sales include sheep as well as cattle. Ancobamba exports cattle above all. The community possesses quite a lot of pasture land and cattle are their main animal product, reared for export. In Ttiomayo, maize accounts for almost three-quarters of agricultural exports, while pigs and cattle account for most animal exports.

Sihuina, in contrast, exports the entire range of its agricultural products, while cattle predominate among its animal exports. It also exports Z-goods in the form of food, principally bread sold at its weekly market. The community earns income from trade by taking valley products – maize, wheat, coca – to the *puna* where they are exchanged for sheep's meat and wool, which in their turn are sold in community markets both in Sihuina and elsewhere.

Huando also exports all its agricultural products in equal proportions, as well as both cattle and sheep. Its mills and trucks provide Z-exports and cater to the surrounding area and, to a lesser extent, to Huando itself. Trading income is derived from the community's own weekly market.

Finally, in Acobamba, 80% of agricultural exports consist of beans, and cattle and sheep are also sold. The community is located at the end of a road, and is therefore a commercial center; its market is a source of trading income for the members of the community.

This list illustrates the diversity of export products both within and between communities. The one exception to this variation is cattle, which clearly constitutes a cash-product produced specifically for export in all the communities, but even then its relative importance varies, thus further underlining the differences between them which were emphasized above.

Imports

In contrast, the structure of imports does not exhibit much variation between communities. Table 4.4 shows that food and drink account for between 37% and 49% of imports. Expenditure on coca, alcohol

Table 4.4 *Structure of monetary imports* (%)

Items	Communities								Total sample	Southern sierra
	JAC	CUL	NIN	ANC	TTI	SIH	HUA	ACO		
Food (coca, alcoholic drinks, cigarettes)	41.9	38.1	42.3	36.9	40.0	45.8	46.1	49.0	43.6	44.8
	(2.9)	(4.3)	(14.5)	(11.6)	(17.1)	(13.1)	(2.7)	(10.2)		
Fuel	3.9	1.9	1.9	2.8	3.2	3.7	4.6	2.4		
Durable goods	0.5	1.1	1.2	0.8	1.5	2.2	0.7	0.7		
Non-durable goods	5.8	4.3	11.2	4.1	9.6	11.0	5.8	7.6		
Clothes and footwear	13.9	16.9	14.1	28.7	24.7	15.4	14.2	11.0	15.6	15.1
Education	6.7	5.7	0.5	3.4	1.6	3.7	3.8	2.7		
Fares	7.9	8.1	5.4	3.7	4.1	4.1	3.0	2.7		
Fiestas	0.7	3.0	7.6	8.4	2.2	4.6	0.5	8.9		
Medicines	2.5	2.5	0.3	1.2	2.4	1.5	6.6	0.7		
Other	1.1	0.1	0.1	0.1	0.1	0.1	2.3	5.3		
Sub-total	84.8	81.7	84.6	90.0	89.3	92.0	87.7	91.0	86.8	87.7
Inputs	9.2	6.5	8.4	5.3	4.8	3.5	7.6	4.1		
Investment	6.0	11.8	7.0	4.7	5.9	4.5	4.7	4.9		
Total	100.0	100.0	100.0	100.0	100.0	100.0	100.0	100.0	100.0	100.0

and cigarettes, which is included under food, is associated with productive activity, since they are used as wage payments in kind, and these are generally considered to be the community's most important expenditures. Table 4.4 shows that these products account for between 3% and 17% of total imports.

A long way behind food and drink, the next most important imports are clothes and footwear, varying between 11% and 29% of the total. Consumer items as a whole account for between 82% and 92% of total imports. Modern inputs to production are of little significance, varying between 4% and 9% of imports. Capital goods are somewhat more important, varying between 5% and 12%, but remain a small item.

This homogeneity of imports compared to the heterogeneity of exports in the communities is explained by the greater homogeneity of their needs, which are restricted to certain types of food, fuel and clothes, and also by their low and relatively uniform levels of income, to which we turn in Chapter 5.

Exchange with other communities

Although there is some monetized exchange between communities, exchange is mostly carried out in kind, and likewise most exchange in kind is accounted for by exchanges with other communities. The estimates of non-monetary exchange can therefore be seen as a measure, albeit an approximate one, of exchange between communities. According to Table 4.1, these exchanges in kind account for a very small proportion of both total production (5% at most, as in the case of Jacantaya) and total exports (7% at most, again in Jacantaya). However, the two communities which are not represented in that table show higher proportions: in Sihuina, 11% of external exchange is accounted for by transactions with other communities, and 23% in Ttiomayo, as shown in Table 4.5. Thus one might conclude that exchange with other communities varies substantially, having an average value of 6% of total external exchange.

Our method of accounting for trading activities may have led, however, to an underestimate of this figure. In communities such as Sihuina, Huando and Acobamba, which have their own weekly markets, much of the trading income which has been classified as 'exports of services' in fact derives from exchange with people from

Table 4.5 *Ratio of non-monetary exchange in peasant communities (soles per year per family and %)*

Community	Value of exports			In-kind share (%)
	Monetary	In kind	Total	
Jacantaya	37,584	2,861	40,445	7.1
Culta	39,771	312	40,083	0.8
Ninamarca	20,813	1,785	22,598	7.9
Ancobamba	17,745	464	18,209	2.5
Ttiomayo	12,530	3,762	16,292	23.1
Sihuina	19,023	2,593	22,616	11.5
Huando	46,484	228	46,712	0.5
Acobamba	26,773	523	27,296	1.9
Sample total				5.6
Southern sierra				5.7

other communities; if one were to include such transactions the proportion of production exchanged with other communities would rise, but not significantly. Moreover, this modification would apply only to communities which have their own markets.

5

The level and structure of peasant income

The information presented in the previous chapter concerning intersectoral relations in peasant communities now permits us to arrive at estimates of the level and structure of income in those communities. In this way we estimate *total peasant income* based on previous understanding of the peasant economy.

The level of total peasant income

One way of calculating peasant income is to consider the value (at market prices) of consumption and investment. As net peasant production is dedicated in part to home consumption and in part to trade, income may be defined as the sum of total consumption and investment, from which the net balance of external exchange must be subtracted. As the value of exports (including transfers) is equal to the value of imports, a second alternative for measuring income is to add to home consumption the value of exports (which would give the net product of $A + P + Z$) and then the value of income from temporary migrations. From this sum we would have to deduct the value of imports of intermediate products which were used to obtain the net product $A + P + Z$. Of course, here we are using the terms imports and exports to refer to goods purchased or sold outside the community.

The third method of calculating income is by way of value added. The estimations of total product $A + P + Z$ and of inputs (domestic and imported) permit us to make this calculation, since the value added is the difference between these two figures. However, income from wages and rent has been estimated directly in the surveys, and thus income from self-employment in $A + P + Z$ was estimated by subtracting out these other components. To the income $A + P + Z$ obtained in this way (value added), we must add the income from

41

temporary migrations in order to arrive at an estimate of *total peasant income*. This income is equal to that calculated by means of final demand. The estimates for the six communities are presented in Tables 5.1–5.3.

To summarize, in the calculation of income we have considered the activities *A*, *P* and *Z* in the community, plus the income from temporary migrations. The allocation of resources to produce goods has been taken account of in its entirety. Production of income-generating (monetary and non-monetary) services is also estimated. The only component of income which is not included is the own-consumption of household services, such as good preparation, gathering of fuel and housing repairs.

The average family income levels estimated vary by community from 47,000 to 82,000 *soles* per year. On a per capita basis this income varies between 12,000 and 20,000 *soles* per year. By comparison, during the period of the survey the legal minimum wage in Lima was between 6,900 and 9,000 *soles* per month, that is, around 100,000 soles annually. The average wage in the manufacturing industry was at that time around 500,000 *soles* annually, and the salary of professionals easily exceeded one million *soles* per year. To put the peasant wages under discussion in a global context, we can use the exchange rate of 200 *soles* per US dollar which was in effect in late 1978 and early 1979. We thus see that the annual family income is approximately 250–400 US dollars, while the annual per capita income is 60–90 dollars. We thus have an estimation of the extreme absolute and relative poverty in which these families live.

Structure of community income

Own-consumption and exchange

Table 5.1 shows that relative proportions of income derived from own-consumption (consumption from own production) and exchange vary among communities, own-consumption representing between 45% and 70% of income. The average value for the six communities is 51% and for the southern sierra 53%. Thus, it may be concluded that own-consumption is approximately half of total income.

This result outlines the importance which the market has for the peasant economy. With this empirical result it is no longer possible to

Table 5.1 *Structure of income of peasant communities: own-consumption and exchange (soles per annum per family)*

Community	Total income	Own-consumption	Exchange A, P, Z		Temporary migration	Imported inputs
JAC	62,441	27,831 (44.6)[a]	27,674	(55.4)	12,772	− 5,836
CUL	68,507	31,175 (45.5)	30,680	(55.5)	9,403	− 2,751
NIN	47,302	26,584 (56.2)	22,456	(43.8)	142	− 1,880
ANC	57,494	40,511 (70.5)	9,751	(29.5)	8,458	− 1,226
HUA	81,518	38,920 (47.7)	42,192	(52.3)	4,520	− 4,114
ACO	60,003	34,245 (57.1)	23,455	(42.9)	3,841	− 1,538
Sample total	67,700	34,406 (50.8)	33,294 (49.2)			
Southern sierra	69,071	36,597 (53.0)	32,474 (47.0)			

[a] Figures in parentheses = percentages.

refer to the peasant economy as 'self-sufficient' or 'dual'. On the contrary, it is an economy well integrated into the rest of the Peruvian economy. Normally when one speaks of countries one refers to an 'open economy' as one in which exports comprise 20–25% of GNP. On the other hand, the peasant economy has always been seen as 'closed', 'self-sufficient', 'outside the market', when in fact it exports almost half of its net product.

How can the varying degree of integration with the market be explained? If the community of Ancobamba is not considered, the range of the proportion of production for home consumption is between 45% and 58%. Ancobamba represents an extreme case, and this may be due to the fact that of the six communities it is the most isolated from highways, being five to six hours' journey from the nearest one. (This is also the case with Sihuina, which may have a structure similar to Ancobamba.) The development of a highway infrastructure is clearly a determining factor in a community's integration with the market. What is surprising is that a third of Ancobamba's income comes from trade with the outside, in spite of its isolation.

Apart from the case of Ancobamba, in the five remaining communities there exists an inverse relation between the level of income and the proportion of it comprised by production for own-consumption. The three communities with a proportion of own-consumption representing between 45% and 48% of income (Jacantaya, Culta and Huando) are the communities with the highest level of peasant income. The two remaining communities have a larger proportion (57–58%) and a lower income level. Nevertheless, these correlations are not very strong, owing to the fact that there are other variables, such as the diversity of resources and the seasonality of agricultural processes, which also influence the degree of economic exchange.

According to productive structure

The data from Table 4.1 allow us to make still another estimate of peasant income. The communities taken as a whole derive income from each of the A, P and Z-activities and the temporary migration of labor. The structure of peasant income broken down into these components is summarized in Table 5.2, which constitutes, in addition, an approach for determining the productive structure of the communities.

Agricultural and livestock activity together represent the largest source of income in the communities, but their relative importance varies considerably: between 43% and 90% of total income.[1] In Jacantaya, where the participation of $A + P$ is the lowest, Z-activities and temporary migration are important components in the income structure. Within the Z-activities the important components are the fishing carried out in Lake Titicaca, together with commerce, particularly that of vegetables. At the other extreme, Ninamarca is a community whose resources are devoted almost exclusively to agriculture and livestock husbandry. Only 10% of total product comes from Z-activities, while temporary migrations do not have

Table 5.2 *Productive structure of the communities (%)*

Community	A	P	Z	Temporary migration	Total
JAC	28.6	14.3	36.6	20.5	100.0
CUL	26.5	47.1	13.7	13.7	100.0
NIN	44.9	44.6	10.2	0.3	100.0
ANC	59.0	21.0	5.3	14.7	100.0
HUA	46.3	17.1	31.1	5.5	100.0
ACO	46.7	20.0	26.9	6.4	100.0
Sample total	43.5	24.5	20.8	11.2	100.0
Southern sierra	46.3	21.9	22.3	9.5	100.0

great importance either. The Z-activities constitute between 5% and 37% of the income in the sample, and are thus in general terms an important source of income. Note that the Z-activities and the temporary migrations together make up close to one-third of peasant income. An implication of this result is that there is an important underestimation in the calculation of rural income when, as in the case of the National Accounts, it is taken only as that emanating from crop and husbandry activities.

By salaries, rents and self-employment

The principal source of income in all the communities is the income from self-employment, as Table 5.3 shows. The proportion varies from 72% to 98% between communities; in other words, normally more than three-quarters of peasant income is from self-employment. The peasant family of today depends to a great deal on the application of its labor to its own resources to generate total income.

Property rents (rents from the use of land, animals and tools) are not very significant.[2] There are no families that make their living primarily in this fashion. Thus, it is wage income which takes second place to self-employment in the composition of total income. There are two job markets to consider: local and external. The income from both markets represents between 4% and 28% of peasant income. If we do not take into account Ninamarca, a community in which almost all income is from self-employment, the proportions of income from wages represent between 17% and 28% of total income in the remaining five communities. In three communities the external market is the most important source of jobs, while in two com-

Table 5.3 *Structure of income of peasant communities : wages, rents and self-employment (soles per annum per family)*

Community	Total income	Local wage employment	Rents	Self-employment	Temporary migrations
JAC	62,441 (100.0)[a]	4,685 (7.5)	72 (0.1)	44,912 (71.9)	12,772 (20.5)
CUL	68,507 (100.0)	3,052 (4.5)	317 (0.5)	55,735 (81.3)	9,403 (13.7)
NIN	47,302 (100.0)	1,045 (2.2)	0 (0.0)	46,115 (97.5)	142 (0.3)
ANC	57,494 (100.0)	1,222 (2.1)	77 (0.1)	47,737 (83.0)	8,458 (14.7)
HUA	81,518 (100.0)	8,683 (10.7)	1,493 (1.8)	66,822 (82.0)	4,520 (5.5)
ACO	60,003 (100.0)	11,050 (18.4)	425 (0.7)	44,687 (74.5)	3,841 (6.4)
Total sample	100.0	7.8	0.8	80.2	11.2
Southern sierra	100.0	8.8	1.0	80.7	9.5

[a] Figures in parentheses = percentages.

munities the local market is of more significance. Employers in the local market are primarily medium-sized landowners who live side by side with peasant families in the community.

Monetary transfers

The final grouping in Table 4.1 refers to monetary transfers. In the communities there exist, on one hand, internal and external transfers; and on the other hand, monetary and in-kind transfers. In all there are thus four forms which transfers among families may take. Direct transfers from the State or from organizations such as the Church have not been estimated. However, neither is important at the level of the community.

In-kind transfers between families within the community include A, P and Z-goods, productive services (especially labor), and monetary transfers which occur on occasions such as marriages and other celebrations. These internal transfers have not been estimated. External transfers *have* been estimated, but only the monetary ones. Estimation of non-monetary external transfers was not possible, due to the difficulties of specifying their quantities and qualities. Nevertheless, it is known that these transfers are very frequent in both directions. The movement of cargo in and out is impressive, above all in communities with access to roads.

The estimates of monetary transfers show the communities as net receivers. The absolute magnitudes vary between communities, as can be seen in Table 5.4. The transfers received come primarily from children who live in urban areas. Cases were also found in which the head of the household lived in another place for occupational reasons and sent money to his family in the community. The transfers out of the community are generally to sons and daughters who study in a city.

Table 5.4 also shows the relative importance of transfers in the peasant economy. As a proportion of total peasant income monetary transfers represent up to 8% or 10%, as in the case of Jacantaya and Huando. For the rest of the communities the figures are quite low. If they are compared with total income from exports (including temporary migrations), monetary transfers increase the purchasing power of exports up to 17% (the case of Jacantaya). For Huando and

Table 5.4   *Money transfers (soles per annum per family)*

Community	Ingress	Egress	Net	% of total income	% of export income
JAC	7,345	871	6,474	10.4	17.2
CUL	3,715	2,100	1,615	2.4	4.1
NIN	0	0	0	0	0
ANC	2,239	417	1,822	3.2	10.3
TTI	267	0	267	n.a.	2.1
SIH	755	0	755	n.a.	4.0
HUA	7,037	450	6,587	8.1	14.2
ACO	564	0	564	1.0	2.1
Sample total					8.0
Southern sierra					7.6

Ancobamba these proportions are 14% and 10% respectively. For the five remaining communities the numbers are not very significant. For the southern sierra, the expansion of these sample results gives a figure of around 8% for monetary transfers as a proportion of total exports.

The monetary budget of the peasant family

The structure of total income shown in the previous section refers to the peasant community, and not to the individual family. For the case of the peasant family, its sources of total income are: A, P and Z-goods (products of self-employment), income obtained from outside employment, such as salaries in the local labor market (W_1) and in markets outside the community (W_2); income from renting land or the means of production (R); and finally, income transfers (T). As is explained in Appendix II, the method of calculation of total peasant income for the community, shown in Table 4.1, was based partly on family income data and partly on global estimates for the community. Thus it was not possible to obtain estimates of *total* peasant income for each family, and in this way arrive at an approximation of the structure of *total* income of the typical peasant family. Although the income structure of the community does not have to be equal to that of the typical family, we will assume here that the differences are not great.[3] Then the result shown in the previous section (in particular, that on average half of total peasant income is monetary) is applicable also to the typical peasant family.

Information on the monetary budget was obtained from all the families and communities. The estimates of monetary income by source, as well as its destination among the categories of monetary expenditure, refer to *gross* income, since allowances have not been made for the family's input purchases for its production.

Structure of gross monetary income

The first conclusion to emerge from Table 5.5 is that the sources of money income are quite diversified. The peasant family has contact with several markets at the same time in order to obtain monetary income. In the second place, the structure of income varies significantly between communities. The third conclusion is a consequence of the earlier ones: all sources of income are important for

Table 5.5 *Structure of monetary income of peasant families (%)*

	Communities								Sample total	Southern sierra
	JAC	CUL	NIN	ANC	TTI	SIH	HUA	ACO		
A	11.8	0.6	58.8	1.5	21.2	13.9	12.8	10.9	10.9	11.1
P	11.7	36.7	23.7	29.2	15.1	21.9	10.7	5.5	20.7	18.7
Z	17.8	15.2	2.7	7.2	0.1	34.2	21.0	15.9	18.5	18.9
W_1	9.0	6.0	5.4	10.3	40.1	10.6	19.3	44.3	15.2	18.3
W_2	21.5	19.7	0.3	22.8	15.1	8.6	9.3	11.6	14.5	13.7
R	0.1	0.3	0.0	0.3	5.0	0.1	0.6	0.0	0.6	0.6
T	17.7	10.0	1.5	16.8	0.7	5.3	10.9	3.4	9.6	8.9
O	10.4	11.5	7.6	11.9	2.7	5.4	15.4	8.4	10.0	9.8
Total	100.0	100.0	100.0	100.0	100.0	100.0	100.0	100.0	100.0	100.0

Note on new symbols: R = rents; T = transfers; O = 'others' (loans, dissavings).

the typical peasant family. This may be seen in the values that appear in the last two columns of Table 5.5.

If we consider only income obtained from economic activity, that is, if we exclude transfers and the category 'others' (loans, dissavings) from Table 5.5, the structure of monetary income of the typical family of the southern sierra is: 14% from the sale of crops, 23% from the sale of livestock, 23% from Z-activities (including commerce), 23% from salaries obtained locally, and 17% from salaries obtained outside the community. Hence, almost 40% of family money income is obtained from the sale of labor. In this sense, and to this extent, the peasant family of today is also a proletarian family.

Structure of gross monetary expenditures
How does the peasant family spend the income which it receives from different sources? Three categories or components of expenditures have been distinguished: intermediate goods and productive services (salaries and rents) for production, capital goods for accumulation, and consumption goods. The consumption goods have been separated into five categories: food and drink, non-durables, clothing and shoes, educational materials and 'others'.

Table 5.6 presents the results of the estimates made from the surveys. As might be expected in this type of estimate concerning

Table 5.6 *Structure of monetary gross expenditure of the peasant family (%)*

Items	Communities								Total sample	Southern sierra
	JAC	CUL	NIN	ANC	TTI	SIH	HUA	ACO		
Inputs	7.7	5.9	7.5	2.8	3.7	3.6	5.8	3.6	5.0	4.7
Services	2.4	1.8	0.2	1.5	3.5	2.3	2.6	1.5	2.1	2.1
Invest-ment	6.3	10.5	5.8	4.1	2.4	3.5	3.9	2.7	5.3	4.6
Food	41.9	37.1	44.6	43.4	40.7	45.1	47.9	55.9	44.2	45.4
Non-durables	10.0	6.4	13.4	8.2	12.6	19.5	12.2	14.0	12.1	12.8
Clothing	10.9	12.4	13.4	22.8	25.4	13.9	12.0	10.0	14.2	14.4
Education	5.7	4.6	0.6	3.0	1.1	4.0	4.6	2.7	3.9	3.8
Others	15.1	21.3	14.5	14.2	10.6	8.1	11.0	9.6	13.2	12.2
Total	100.0	100.0	100.0	100.0	100.0	100.0	100.0	100.0	100.0	100.0

family expenses, one conclusion is that the structure of expenses is well diversified, as it includes many different products and services. However, it may be seen from the aggregated data in Table 5.6 that the category of food is the dominant one in the structure of expenditures. The typical peasant family spends 37–56% of its budget on food, depending on the community. The categories that follow in importance are non-durables, and clothing and shoes. The remaining categories, including the money spent on inputs and productive services, are less significant. Nor is a large part of the monetary budget spent on investments. The second conclusion is that the structure of monetary expenditures is more homogeneous for the different communities than that of income. The order of importance of the different expenditure categories is quite similar in all of the communities.

The typical peasant family of the southern sierra allocates around 5% of its expenditures to production inputs, and somewhat less than 2% to productive services (salaries and rents). In other words, less than 7% of expenditures goes toward production. A smaller proportion, around 4%, is spent on capital goods. This means that approximately 90% of expenditures goes toward consumer goods (as seen in the last column of Table 5.6). Thus, the peasant family allocates the greater part of its monetary income to the acquisition of consumer goods. The family's accumulation is very much reduced, as only a small part of its monetary budget is destined for investment. Net investment is even smaller, almost nil, as much of investment expenditure (in animals and tools) is replacement. The low expenditure in hiring labor is the result of our definition of peasant family: a family that does not hire labor. The proportion spent on modern inputs is also relatively small and clearly indicates the limited incorporation of modern inputs into the production process.

Almost half of the peasant family's expenditures on consumer goods is for food. This category includes both processed and un-processed products, of urban and rural origin respectively. The monetary expenditures on this latter group are fairly small. There are of course families who purchase potatoes, maize and barley when their own harvest is insufficient, or who buy meat, eggs and milk. There are also families who spend money on foods processed in the community (Z-goods such as *chicha* and *chuño*). However, all of these products together do not represent a significant part of monetary expenditure. The principal food purchases are of six processed products of urban origin (salt, sugar, cooking oil, ice, noodles and flour) and two products of rural origin but which are brought in from outside the sierra (coca and cane liquor). The expenditure on these two products, together with cigarettes, is associated principally with work. They constitute part of the payment in kind for wage labor or for reciprocal work within the community.

There are two types of non-durable goods of great importance: combustibles (kerosene and candles) and cleaning articles (soap and laundry detergent). The category 'clothing' includes clothing for the entire family, such as pants, shirts, shoes (normally of synthetic materials), hats and skirts (the traditional *pollera*).

Peasant differentiation and forms of entrance into the market system

Examining the monetary budget, we have shown in the previous section the distinct ways in which a *typical* peasant family enters into the market economy. In each community there are differences between families as to the form that their incorporation into the market takes. Not all families participate in the same markets and derive their income or carry out their expenditures in the same way. There are income differences in the communities and the question is whether the poorest peasant families enter into the market in a way distinct from those who are less poor. In other words, are there significant differences in the structure of income between families belonging to different economic strata within a community? In this section we present some empirical results related to this issue.

Inequality in monetary income

The most trustworthy result from the empirical point of view relates to the monetary income and expenditures of the families. As indicated above, the income from production for own-consumption has been estimated for several products taking the community as a whole, but not for the individual families. For this reason it is not possible to analyze inequalities in *total* income between families.

One possibility is to measure the inequality in terms of monetary income only. This measure is quite useful as a quantitative approximation of the degree of inequality. We would expect monetary income to increase with total family income, and at an increasing rate. Thus, income inequality is overestimated when measured only in terms of monetary income. Table 5.7 presents various indicators of inequality. As can be seen, inequality is fairly pronounced, even taking into account the bias indicated above. For example, the ratio of the percentage of income received by the top quartile to that received by the bottom quartile has a magnitude of between 4 and 13, depending on the community. Thus, in addition to a low level of income in the communities, there is a considerable variation in level from one family to another. Clearly the peasant communities do not constitute a homogeneous mass of poverty. Given the income inequality, the question of how families from different economic strata enter the market takes on special importance.

Patterns of monetary income in the peasant communities

It is important to study the family income structure by economic stratum. In this way we can learn which are the most important sources of income for the poorest peasant families, and for those that are relatively better-off. Nevertheless, it would make little sense to speak of the most important sources of income for poor (or rich) families in general, when we have shown in previous sections that the

Table 5.7 *Inequality in family monetary incomes*

| Community | Coefficient of | | | Income share of | |
	Variation	Gini	Skewness	Lower quartile (%)	Upper quartile (%)
JAC	64.3	0.33	1.3	10	51
CUL	64.1	0.34	1.2	9	48
NIN	86.8	0.36	2.9	8	51
ANC	132.9	0.50	3.7	5	61
TTI	57.2	0.29	1.7	11	45
SIH	80.4	0.36	2.8	8	48
HUA	130.3	0.53	2.8	5	64
ACO	113.7	0.47	3.5	7	59

sources of income vary greatly from one community to another. For example, in the community of Culta agricultural monetary income is insignificant, and thus is not of importance for any stratum. In Ninamarca, on the other hand, agricultural monetary income is very important, and may have a varying relative importance between economic strata.

For the reasons discussed above, instead of showing income structure by stratum in each community, we have opted to examine whether or not there exist generalized income patterns by stratum in all the communities. Is agricultural monetary income, for example, greater in the upper strata, i.e. does it increase with the family's total income level *independent* of the community? The *level* of agricultural monetary income will depend on the community with which we are dealing, due to the above-mentioned differences in sources of income between communities. However, the slope of the line relating agricultural monetary income to total income may be similar (if not in magnitude, at least in sign) between communities. The usefulness of this procedure is that it permits us to identify the types of monetary income which vary negatively with total income, and which are thus the most important for the poorer families. It may also be of interest to know which types of monetary income vary positively with total income, and whether these have the same or lesser importance for the poorer families as for the more prosperous ones. We already know that all income sources except rent are important for the typical family. Now we can determine the relative importance of different income sources by stratum.

In order to carry out the proposed analysis we have designed a regression model of the following form:

$$Y_j = \alpha_j + \sum_i \beta_{ij} X_i + \gamma_j Y$$

where Y_j is the monetary income of type j, Y is the total monetary income of the family, and the X_is are dummy variables for each of the eight communities. With this specification we maintain the difference in income levels by type between communities, calculated by taking the differences in the intercepts. We have considered six types of income, each representing different markets and mechanisms of market entry. The six types are income from agriculture, livestock, commerce, unskilled wage labor in the community, skilled wage labor in the community and wage labor outside the community. Income from Z-good sale was not analyzed due to its specific character for each community. The model was applied to all the families in the sample.

Three equations were specified in addition to the one presented above: one utilizing the original data in log–linear form, and two others using deflated values of the variables in conjunction with the two functional forms. As the survey was conducted during a period of marked inflation in Peru (around 60% annually), correcting the nominal values of the variables by deflating with a price index seemed a proper step before comparing the communities. The time difference between the first and last community surveys was eight months.

The results of the regression analysis are shown in Table 5.8. In view of the fact that the results using deflated values for the variables were similar to those using the original ones, only these latter equations are shown. In general the equations show the existence of a significant relation between a specific type of income and total income. All of the regression coefficients except one are significant at the 0.05 level. Nevertheless, the R^2 values are not very high. This is the case in particular for income from temporary migration. The results suggest that there exists a positive relationship between total monetary income and all sources of income except that from unskilled labor in the local market. The positive relationship with cropping and livestock husbandry monetary income can be explained by the fact that the richer peasant families have a much larger marketable surplus than the poor families, because they have more land and animals. This

Table 5.8 *Summary of the regression analysis*

	Regression coefficient		Global	
Variable	Value	F-value	R^2 (adjusted)	F-value
Linear				
Agriculture (A)	0.113	108	0.370	22
Livestock (P)	0.081	35	0.243	12
Commerce	0.308	243	0.494	36
Wages – local (W_1)	− 0.015	9	0.369	22
Wages – local (skilled)	0.101	98	0.270	14
Wages – external	0.028	5[a]	0.108	5
Logs				
Agriculture (A)	0.865	12	0.400	26
Livestock (P)	1.851	36	0.159	8
Commerce	2.004	57	0.271	15
Wages – local (W_1)	− 1.229	21	0.245	13
Wages – local (skilled)	0.295	1[b]	0.012	1[b]
Wages – external	0.859	7	0.109	6

[a] Non-significant at the 1% level.
[b] Non-significant at the 5% level.

would be true even if the proportion of production for own-consumption were equal for rich and poor families (which may not be the case). It is to be expected that production for own-consumption (consisting primarily of food crops) diminishes as a proportion of total income in the upper economic strata.

The fact that monetary income from commerce increases with the level of total monetary income indicates that the relatively better-of peasant families are heavily involved in this activity. Personal contacts, knowledge of Spanish, available working capital: all make the wealthier families much more suited for commerce. Poor families, on the other hand, carry out *small-scale commerce*, thus obtaining a lower income from these activities than is the case with the rich peasant families. In some communities the latter are even able to make selling trips to the large cities carrying their wares in trucks.

The other income category which is positively related to total income is the income from skilled labor in the community. Artisans, particularly bricklayers, obtain relatively high salaries in the labor market, and the wealthier families derive more income from these activities.

With respect to wage income from unskilled labor in the local market, the results show that this type of income is less in *absolute* terms among the rich families than among the poor ones. The wealthier families do not work for wages in the community; on the contrary, given their resources, many of them are demanders of casual labor whereas the more impoverished families are the suppliers of labor. The logical question is, do these poorer families also obtain more income from temporary migrations than do their better-off counterparts? Although the statistical result is weaker, there are indications that income from seasonal migrations varies positively with total monetary income. This source is relatively more important for the middle and upper strata. One would expect that the rich families would have sufficient resources and would not need to migrate, while the poor families would. Nevertheless, these results show the opposite. One possible explanation is that it is skilled labor (which the poor families do not have) which is exported. This 'skill' refers not only to a particular occupation, such as carpenter, brickmason, weaver or musician, but also to 'cultural skills'. A knowledge of the Spanish language, of how to read and write, of how to conduct oneself in cities and in the valleys where modern farming methods are practiced – all of these are required, and are found mostly among families in the upper economic strata.

There is an additional factor which is required to migrate seasonally: working capital. In order to absent himself from the farm for two or three months, the head of the household must have enough funds to cover the expenses of his family during that period, as well as the costs of traveling, lodging and looking for work. Poorer families obviously have less of this working capital than richer ones. It is for this reason that the debt peonage system (*enganche* in Spanish, literally 'hooking') of intermediaries in rural labor markets is so important. The contractor (*enganchador*) provides the peasant with capital, in the form of a cash advance. A relatively prosperous peasant family would certainly not wait for advances before migrating temporarily.

All of the above leads us to the conclusion that the richer families in the peasant communities derive more income from *all* sources than the poorer ones, with the exception of wage labor within the community. This is due to the fact that richer families have access to a large quantity of *all* the resources which exist in each community.

From the regression analysis we may also make inferences regarding the *proportions* of total income consisting of given types of income, and how they vary with total income. In the case of the logarithmic regressions it is sufficient to look at the value of the regression coefficient, since this is equivalent to the elasticity coefficient. From Table 5.8 we infer that the proportion of total income made up of agricultural monetary income diminishes as the level of total income increases. The same thing occurs with wage income from the communal labor market. In both these cases the elasticities are less than one. For income from livestock and commerce the elasticities are greater than one, indicating that this income makes up a larger share of total income as the latter increases.

In conclusion, there exist clear income patterns among peasant families, in spite of the differences in the sources of income between families. Wage income from work in the community has a greater absolute and relative importance among the poorer families, regardless of the community concerned. The same may be said of agricultural monetary income, except that the importance is only in relative terms. On the other hand, monetary income from livestock and commerce has a greater absolute and relative importance for the families of the upper strata, independently of the community. These two activities generate income primarily for the relatively wealthier peasants. Wage income from external markets is relatively more important for middle and upper strata.

6

The economic behavior of the peasant family

Even though peasant families are organized in communities, the economic decisions that they make concerning the use of their resources and labor are fundamentally family decisions. The results presented up to now show that the peasant family is at the same time a production and a consumption unit. It is of interest to know the essential elements that determine the economic behavior of the peasant family. What are the principles guiding its economic actions? What is its economic rationality? From the answers to these questions, we can derive propositions about the mechanisms that govern the allocation of peasant family labor to alternative uses and the reactions to market prices. These are the themes that we shall attempt to develop in this chapter.

Portfolio of activities and risk-aversion

Any economic theory which attempts to explain the behavior of the peasant family of the sierra must include as an essential element the problem of risk. There are two reasons for this. First, practically all the economic activities of the sierra peasants are subject to risk and uncertainty. Agriculture in the sierra is certainly a tremendously risky activity. Since there is normally no irrigation, dependence on rainfall is complete. The absence of rain, its appearance at the wrong time, or its over-abundance (creating floods and avalanches) affect production significantly. At certain altitudes, frost and hail are climatic factors which also affect production negatively and in an unpredictable manner. To these problems of nature we must add others, such as diseases. Livestock production also confronts significant risks, such as falls (due to the rugged nature of the terrain) and strayings. The production of Z-goods is in itself perhaps less risky, but since in most cases it depends on crop and livestock inputs, or on trading activities, it does not escape having a strong chance component. Finally, the incursion into the external labor market is at least as risky as the other activities. The possibility of not finding employment, of losing one's pay, of falling ill, are all clear examples of this problem. The peasants who do not go out looking for jobs often say of those who do: 'They only go looking for illness and come back sick.'

In the second place, the peasant families of the sierra are poor. It is to be expected that the poor family will have an aversion to risk, avoiding as far as possible endangering its income. A large loss of income would mean economic disaster. The poor family confronted with alternatives open to risk will thus prefer a small loss in its income to a small chance of suffering a large loss.

Given the risk involved in the production and exchange activities carried out by a peasant family in the sierra, a hypothesis concerning its economic behavior could be stated in the following way: the peasant family tries to assure, with the least risk, the attainment of a bundle of commodities which is culturally determined.

In the case that production and exchange processes show a trade-off between average income and security for the peasant family, the way to minimize risk is by means of a combination of activities; that is, by means of a diversified portfolio of resources and activities. This diversification, as shown in the present study, is precisely one of the characteristics of the peasant families and, thus, is entirely consistent with the hypothesis put forward.

The preference for diversification of activities is clearly revealed in an affirmation made by a Jacantaya peasant: 'Our agricultural production is not guaranteed, due to problems of weather against which we are defenseless. In order not to run this risk we could complement our activities with other jobs in artisanry or some industry. We would thus like to have a factory or workshop in order to work. Perhaps in this way we could improve our situation.'

Portfolio diversification does not refer only to different activities (A-P-Z-L), however. It refers also to diversification within an activity itself. In the case of agriculture we observed that the peasant family sows many different crops, and has numerous small parcels of land. Why does the family not specialize in a few crops? Why does it farm such tiny, scattered parcels? A crop portfolio implies for the peasant family the acquisition of parcels in different ecological zones, in order to have access to more resources and a larger set of production possibilities. As the negative effects of climate and plagues are not the same in all the ecological zones, the probability of *all* crops turning out badly becomes significantly reduced.

Even within the same ecological zone, the peasants take advantage of the existence of special micro-climates to minimize risk by planting on several parcels. For example, frosts do not affect an entire area equally: flat and open fields are affected more than sheltered areas at the foot of hills or mountains. A good illustration of this fact comes from the statement of a peasant from the community of Culta: 'Since the frost falls mostly in the open fields but not on the slopes, if we sow only in the flat places the frost can wipe out everything and we are then left without anything to eat. So it is better to sow in different spots. That way, you win some, and you lose some.' To the number of parcels which the peasant uses in his crop portfolio we must add parcels which are lying fallow and will be used for crop rotation. The number of parcels which the farmer possesses is thus larger than the number utilized, which is in turn explained by the diversification in the crop portfolio.[1]

It is very probable that the uncertainty associated with agriculture and livestock limits the diffusion of modern inputs. In the sierra it is not a question of applying fertilizers and automatically obtaining a good crop. Frost, hail and drought can cause even fertilized crops to fail. A peasant from Huando sums up this problem in a very clear way: 'Several peasants have obtained loans from the Agrarian Bank to buy fertilizers and pesticides and have suffered crop failures due to bad weather. They are scared now to ask for loans again.'[2]

Among the economic activities open to the peasant family, not all of them have the same degree of uncertainty. If this is so, the alternatives of average net income and its degree of uncertainty open to peasant families will vary for each mix of *A-P-Z-L* activities. A hypothesis on this issue would be to say that the way in which agriculture and livestock production is organized in peasant communities suggests that these activities (*A-P*), taken *jointly*, have a lower degree of uncertainty (or variance). The mix of resources, crops, parcels and types of animals indicates a very complex portfolio of activities in agriculture and livestock production so that the risk of a complete failure in production is greatly reduced. Also the risk in exchange is lower because part of the *A-P* output is for own-consumption.

In order to illustrate the previous argument, suppose a peasant family specializes in the production of a single crop. If this crop fails the family will face an economic disaster; but even if it does not fail, this crop must be exchanged for other consumption goods. The attainment of the basket of consumption goods is now subject to the results of market exchange. Producing, in part, for own-consumption is a way to reduce the risk in exchange. Hence, agriculture and livestock production taken *together* reduce the risk, in production and exchange, to assure the family's given basket of consumption.

A consequence of this risk-aversion behavior is that agriculture and livestock production are given a priority in the allocation of family resources, particularly of family labor. These resources are not allocated to the different activities so as to maximize average income. The allocation is *biased* toward more resources put into livestock production as compared to the allocation that maximizes average income; but risk will be reduced. It is in this sense that we can talk about a *hierarchy* in the use of resources as another characteristic of the economic behavior of the peasant family.

This theoretical result is consistent with an answer frequently obtained from peasants when they are asked why they do not migrate temporarily to work in other places where wages are comparatively high: 'I do not go elsewhere to work because I do not have time.' This is meant to indicate that crop and livestock tasks do not leave enough time for migration to external labor markets. In many cases the peasants do not even know what wages are paid in nearby cities or valleys. Their holding of land offers them an income which is lower, but more secure.

Agricultural seasonality and the allocation of family labor

Agricultural activity is seasonal, but in the particular case of the sierra this seasonality is quite marked, due to the fact that most of the land is dependent on rainfall for its water. The profile of agricultural seasonality which is shown in Figure 6.1 corresponds to what has generally been observed in the communities under study. Turning over the soil on lands which have been lying fallow takes place in March and April, months in which the rainy season is ending. This is particularly true of lands under collective rotation (the *laymi*). Planting begins in August or September, with the arrival of the first rains, and lasts until November of December. Once the planting is carried out, the calendar of cultural practices is practically de-

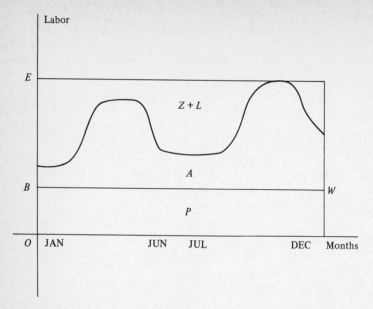

Figure 6.1 Seasonality in peasant communities of the sierra

termined; these are carried out principally between September and January. The harvest calendar is also determined by the planting date, the peak months being May and June. The end result is that July–September and January–April are periods of little agricultural activity.

The agricultural calendar mentioned is certainly a simplification of what is observed in each community. There are important differences between communities in the timing of agricultural activities. This may be due to the mixture of crops, the particular ecological zones, the micro-climates or the availability of water for irrigation. Irrigated lands give two crops per year in the *quechua* and *yunga* regions; in the high regions this is less common, because of the strong frosts between May and July. For this reason, the profile shown in Figure 6.1 is indicative only of a 'typical' agriculture cycle in the sierra. In this figure agricultural seasonality includes the labor requirements of livestock production (equal to *OB*). To simplify matters, we have assumed that there is no significant seasonality in livestock production (although some activities such as shearing have a fixed calendar).

The profile shown in the diagram refers to a typical family, although it could also represent an entire community. If a community has OE workers, it can supply itself with the labor it needs even in periods of peak requirement. There will, however, be seasonal unemployment in agricultural activities. If there are more than OE units of labor the community is overpopulated, and the excess population can move elsewhere without causing a decline in crop and livestock production. If there are fewer than OE units of labor, the community has a deficit. In the first case we would observe temporary migrations outside the community even in peak periods of agricultural activity. The second case would be consistent with peasant immigration from other communities, particularly in periods such as the harvest. If Figure 6.1 is taken to refer to a peasant family, the vertical axis measures the size of the family labor supply and the curve then represents labor requirements for the quantity of resources which the family economic unit has at its disposal.

How is family labor assigned to A, P, L and Z-activities? Consistent with the risk-averse behavior discussed earlier, agricultural seasonality seems to be the labor allocation mechanism. It is only once the crop and livestock activities are concluded that the peasant family takes decisions concerning other uses of the family labor force, whether it is to employ itself in the production of Z-goods or to enter the job market. Z-goods thus constitute complementary, not competitive, activities with respect to agriculture and livestock in the countryside. In order to be complementary, these activities should not be seasonal (i.e. one should be able to start and finish them at any time); or, if they are seasonal, they should have a cycle opposite to that of the crops. Most Z-activities comply with one of these requirements. Some examples of the first category are textiles and commerce; of the second, construction which is carried on outside the rainy season (between harvest and the next sowing), as well as the processing of food which takes place after planting and before harvest.

In the peasant communities almost everything has its 'season'. There is a specific form of work organization during the year, which imposes a certain rhythm and sequence on family labor. The most important factor in defining this rhythm and sequence is the agricultural calendar. There are two reasons for this. First, when the schedules for L and Z-activities are flexible, these can be postponed. The stages of the agricultural process, on the other hand, cannot be postponed without risking a loss in production. Secondly, when a number of activities coincide in their calendar, the *A* and *P* ones have priority for the reasons explained earlier.

The hypothesis of risk-aversion and the existence of a marked agricultural seasonality together imply that the production of *Z*-goods is not affected in a significant way by crop and livestock production, but rather by the salaries that prevail in the job market. In the peasant family the allocation of labor to *Z*-activities and to wage labor refers basically to the use of off-season labor. This means that the peasant can dedicate himself only partially to crop and livestock activity and still consider it to be the most important activity in his effort to assure a subsistence income for himself and his family. Even though he may be only a part-time peasant, that is his principal identity. The plot of land gives him a measure of economic security.

The central hypotheses concerning the economic behavior of the peasant family have clear implications for its entrance into the labor market. In the following two sections we present the empirical evidence.

The labor market in the community

The peasant family does not carry out its productive activity in isolation from the rest of the families of the community. As we indicated earlier, we observe three systems of exchange of labor services in the community: (a) reciprocity; (b) payment in kind; and (c) monetary wages.

The system of reciprocity, called *ayni*, has an important requirement for its functioning: the net balance for each family should be zero. If a family has contracted five peasants for its planting, it has the obligation of working five days for the others. If all families had the same resources, they would all have to work five days in exchange, and in this way the entire harvest would be finished with a perfect communal labor balance. However, the existence of significant peasant differentiation makes this communal balance imperfect. There are families with a labor deficit or surplus. In addition, the richest peasants will always prefer to contract laborers rather than practice *ayni*, because they consider their opportunity cost to be very high. There will also be some households (those consisting of widows, for example) that cannot pay for services received with their own labor. Finally, in every community there is a group of families owning medium-sized farms, whose greater economic resources and cultural differences with respect to the peasants set them apart. In the language of the peasants (and of the Peruvian novelist Arguedas), these are the vecinos ('neighbors'). These 'neighbors' also require workers. From all this a labor market emerges in the community.

Payments for work done in the communities (*total* wages) have two components. One is the wage proper, and the other is a payment in goods defined according to the socio-cultural matrix of the community, and considered a 'right'. This 'right' usually includes food, coca, *aguardiente* (cane liquor) and cigarettes. A typical wage contract offered by an employer would include as a 'right' two meals, a fistful (around an ounce) of coca, a quarter-bottle of *aguardiente* and one or two cigarettes to each peasant for a day's work. Even if wages are paid in kind (for example, work at harvest is paid with part of the crop, and at planting with seed), the other non-monetary payment ('the right') is still made. In Huando, where the monetary component of *total* wages is more important than in the other communities, the non-monetary component was estimated equal in value to the monetary one when evaluated at market prices.

In the case of *ayni* only the non-monetary part of the wage is paid. In addition, where the peasants concerned are very poor, they reduce the quantity of the goods in 'rights' or they eliminate certain items (food, for example, agreeing that each worker will provide his own). On the other hand, in the *minka* system, the total wage consists primarily of the 'right' to the non-monetary payment. Sometimes it includes payment in kind, but this is not common. As the employer does not return the labor received, as in the *ayni* system, the non-monetary payment is much greater in quantity and quality than when there is also payment of wage proper either in cash or in kind. Usually the worker's family also receives food and care. If any balance remains in the peasant's favor, the employer will compensate for it with services at a later date. This latter point implies that *minka* is typically a relationship between families from the upper strata (including 'neighbors') and poor peasants, while *ayni* is carried out mainly among peasants from the lower strata.

The local labor market exists principally for adult men, as the opportunities for women and children are much fewer. Only in Huando, where there exist various families of 'neighbors', is there an important market for domestic help, i.e. women and children. The most important source of employment for women and children is helping with the harvest, where wage is paid in kind. The principal role of these family members is not to obtain wage income directly for the family (although as we shall see, *many* children do migrate seasonally). The main responsibility of the women and children is to take care of the productive unit (the family's crop and livestock enterprises) so that the adult man is reasonably free to earn wage income elsewhere.

Daily money wages vary significantly within the same community and during a given month. This variance can be explained in part by differences in the quality and quantity of the 'rights' (the non-monetary wages). Thus, for example, the monetary wage with food is less than the monetary wage without food. But in Huando, for example, the monetary wage with food varied between 80 and 120 *soles* daily. Part of this difference is due to the slowness of the labor market's adjustment to inflation. In any case, the money wage differences also reflect to a great extent the personal relations that prevail in the community, and the long-term 'balances' between individuals. In addition, the fluidity in the adjustment of the labor market to new money wage levels appears to depend also on the role that personal relations play in the market. Personal relations make market adjustments less fluid.

Employers in the community frequently complain that there is a shortage of labor in the community, particularly during periods of peak agricultural activity. One of the 'neighbors' indicated that when he needs 10 laborers he contacts 15 'just to be safe'. The peasant family who has extra labor after self-employment in the plot has various alternatives, such as self-employment in Z-activities or migration outside the community. The opportunity cost is not zero during the off-season for the peasant family's labor force. The fundamental mechanism attracting these peasants to the local labor market must be increases in wages. Nevertheless, seasonal variations in monetary wages are not observed in the community. The adjustment clearly comes from the increase in payment in kind or in rights to goods. At harvest time, for example, a common practice is payment in kind of an amount of the product which has a greater market value than the average monetary wage. The different components of the *total* wage offer considerable flexibility for adjustments.

One reason not to increase monetary wages in periods of labor scarcity is the employer's awareness of the downward inflexibility (or 'stickiness') of wages. Huando provides a clear example. Here the employers prefer to hire workers from neighboring communities during the harvest season. They are paid an amount which exceeds the going money wage in Huando or the other communities, because they are in the area only temporarily. The workers from Huando are not paid more, because 'one mustn't spoil them', as employers say.

Daily money wages also vary from one community to another. The average wage for adult men during the period of the survey was 30 *soles* in Sihuina, 60 *soles* in Ninamarca, 80 *soles* in Ancobamba and 100 *soles* in Huando, Acobamba, Jacantaya and Culta.

The labor supply obviously comes from the family units with a net labor surplus. This supply will be determined by opportunity costs: products that can be obtained with self-employment principally in the production of Z-goods and the net wages which can be obtained by temporary migration outside the community. In this analysis we must note that, because of the hypothesis of risk-aversion (and the hierarchy in labor allocation), crop and livestock production do not enter fully into the calculation of the opportunity cost. On the other hand, since *ayni* is a way of organizing mutually aided production by means of self-employment, it has no implications for the communal labor market. Quantities of labor demanded and supplied are always equal under the *ayni* system.

The external labor market

The temporary migrations which peasants make to labor markets outside the community have the characteristic of being seasonal. The data presented in Table 6.1 are a clear indication of this fact. When we compare the number of person-days of temporary migration by month with the average for the year, we see that the months when the former is greater than the latter are always grouped together. For instance, the greatest migrations in Jacantaya are in the months of November–February and May–June. The second characteristic of the temporary migrations is that the periods when this activity is most intense coincide with the periods of least intensity in agricultural activity. In all the communities the periods of greatest migration are in the summer (December–May) and winter (June–August) months. The few cases in which the greatest migration occurs in other months (though always adjacent to the ones mentioned) are due to the specific agricultural calendar of the respective community. There are com-

Table 6.1 *Temporary migrations (number of days per family)*

Months	JAC	CUL	NIN	ANC	TTI	SIH	HUA	ACO
				Communities				
Jan.	8.0*	4.0*	0.5	4.5*	11.0*	2.2*	4.8*	1.1
Feb.	7.2*	4.4*	0.0	4.5*	4.7*	2.2*	4.3*	3.3*
March	4.3	4.8*	0.0	4.5*	3.3*	2.2*	2.9*	4.0*
April	2.6	0.9	0.5	3.8*	0.7	0.7	2.3	2.5*
May	9.3*	0.9	0.5	1.5	0.0	0.0	0.8	1.5
June	10.6*	5.0*	0.0	0.8	0.4	0.0	0.7	0.9
July	4.7	5.9*	0.0	3.4*	0.7	0.7	0.7	0.9
Aug.	2.0	4.0*	0.0	8.8*	0.2	0.7	5.0*	2.5*
Sept.	2.6	0.9	1.0	1.5	0.6	0.0	3.0*	2.5*
Oct.	4.3	2.0	0.0	1.9	2.1	0.8	0.7	2.8*
Nov.	10.1*	1.2	0.0	1.1	2.0	0.8	1.4	1.7
Dec.	8.4*	2.1	0.0	1.6	3.9*	0.7	2.9*	1.1
Total	75	43	2.5	39	30	14	29	24
Monthly average	6.2	3.6	0.2	3.2	2.5	1.1	2.5	2.0

Note: Values with asterisk indicate a higher value than the monthly average.

munities that have an agricultural calendar slightly ahead of or behind the rest.

The evidence presented in Table 6.1 appears to be sufficiently solid to conclude that temporary migrations are, indeed, *seasonal migrations*. They are dependent on agricultural seasonality. This evidence is consistent with the hypothesis presented above of *hierarchy* in the selection of activities, where crop and livestock activities have priority.

Table 6.1 also shows the average number of person-days of migration from each community. The lowest average is in Nina-marca, with 2.5 days; the highest ones are Jacantaya (75 days), Culta (43) and Ancobamba (39). For the sierra as a whole, our estimate is that the typical peasant family utilizes 34 person-days of its labor supply for temporary migration. Since the common pattern is for the head of the household to migrate, we may conclude that the head of the household is typically absent for more than one month per year. If we suppose that the total number of effective workdays is 270–80, this indicates that around 12% of the available labor time of the head of the household (i.e. of the adult male) is allocated to obtaining income by means of entrance into external job markets.[3]

What type of markets are these to which peasants migrate? The places of migration have been classified in two ways. The first set of criteria concerned whether the market was regional or extra-regional. 'Regional' is defined as meaning that the place of employment was located in the same province or 'zone' as the community. The idea was to distinguish between better-known, visible markets (familiar to the majority of the peasants), and markets which were farther away and less well known. Another characteristic of the regional market is that it has a lower cost of entry than the extra-regional one. The empirical results show that most of the migrants go to the extra-regional markets. As Table 6.2 indicates, 27% of the heads of households migrated to extra-regional labor markets, and 11% to regional ones.

Secondly, the destination of the migrants was classified according to whether it was a rural or urban zone. The idea was to measure in this way the importance of rural and urban labor markets for the peasant economy (independent of being regional or extra-regional). Table 6.2 shows that the rural markets have the greater importance,

Table 6.2 *Destination of temporary migrants to external labor markets* (%)

Community	Regional	Extra-regional	Rural	Urban	Various[a]	House-hold with no migrants
			Destination			
JAC	5.6	47.2	27.8	19.5	2.8	41.7
CUL	25.0	27.5	17.5	30.0	5.0	40.0
NIN	9.7	3.2	12.9	0	0	87.1
ANC	40.0	10.0	15.0	32.5	2.5	45.0
TTI	2.8	33.3	36.1	2.8	2.8	58.3
SIH	2.4	24.4	24.4	2.4	0	73.2
HUA	0	30.9	7.1	19.0	0	69.0
ACO	7.7	28.2	28.2	5.1	0	64.1
Total sample	11.7	27.5	19.5	16.8		57.7
Southern sierra	10.6	27.0	20.0	15.0		60.1

[a] Cases of migrants going to more than one destination.

although the difference is not as pronounced as in the regional–extra-regional distinction. Although there are some differences between communities in terms of the more relevant external job markets, for the peasant families as a whole the conclusions are clear: the largest group enters extra-regional and rural labor markets.

Finally, Table 6.2 shows the proportion of families in which no member migrated temporarily in the year preceding the survey. This proportion varies between communities, ranging from 40–42% for Culta and Jacantaya to 87% in Ninamarca. These proportions coincide with the ordering of the number of days spent as migrants. From this we can conclude that there are some communities which migrate more than others, and that there are no families which specialize in migrating, independently of the community in which they live. If this were the case, we would observe little relation between communities as far as the proportion of days spent as migrants and the proportion of families who migrate. For the southern sierra as a whole, 40% of the families have at least one member who has temporarily left the community in search of work.

The principal activity which the migrating peasants enter is agriculture. Of all who left during the year, 54% worked in this sector. Of these, three-quarters obtained employment working with crops destined for the national markets, such as rice, vegetables and fruit (on the coast), and coca and lumber (in the *selva*, or eastern jungle). The remaining 25% worked in export agriculture: cotton on the coast and coffee in the *selva*, as shown in Table 6.3. The other important occupation for the migrating peasants is construction, where 33% of them found employment. The urban service sector accounted for 19% – unloading trucks, working as street vendors, domestic servants or waiters and waitresses. Two additional activities with less importance are mining and handicrafts (including musicians).

In sum, the labor markets through which most peasants pass are those related to agriculture and construction. This pattern of migration well reflects the skills of the peasants. On the other hand, the employment they obtain is principally on small and medium-sized farms, or with small firms. One reason they do not work in large enterprises (the 'modern sector') is that these usually ask for work papers and identification documents, which the peasants usually do not have. ('I can only work on small construction jobs – in the big ones they ask for papers'; 'I always go to the same place – since they

Table 6.3 *Employment sectors of temporary migrants (number of persons)*

| Community | Agriculture | | Construc-tion | Servi-ces | Handi-crafts | Mining | Total[a] |
	Domestic	Exports					
JAC	13	2	2	5	0	0	21
CUL	6	0	9	5	0	0	19
ANC	5	1	11	1	6	1	20
TTI	15	0	1	1	0	0	15
SIH	4	2	1	0	0	0	7
HUA	2	3	4	4	0	3	14
ACO	1	8	0	3	1	0	12
Total	46	16	28	19	7	4	108
Total sample	217	76	179	105	30	26	542
(%)	(40.0)	(14.0)	(33.0)	(19.4)	(5.5)	(4.8)	(100.0)

Note: No data were available for Ninamarca.
[a] 'Total' does not add up because the same migrants can have employment in more than one sector.

already know me they give me work, while others ask to see my documents', are common peasant statements.) One consequence of this is that even to enter labor markets the peasant becomes dependent on personal relations. In effect, the majority of the peasants look for employment through relatives, persons from the same community, or acquaintances. In this sense they rarely actually 'go out to look for work'. Some peasants revealed to us that in order to work with large enterprises, they had to pay the person in charge of hiring. This cost, added to the cost of obtaining work papers, imposes additional barriers on the entrance of peasants into the 'formal' labor market.

Another cost that must be faced by the peasant who migrates is the financing necessary for leaving the community. A three-month absence involves leaving the family enough cash for everyday expenses, and having enough for carrying out the trip. The costs of transportation and lodging, clothing or tools necessary for the job, the days of waiting before getting the job and before receiving the first pay all imply the necessity of having a 'working capital' in order to obtain work. The amount of this 'working capital' has been estimated in the survey. In the majority of the cases, the answer varied between 500 and 3,000 *soles* depending on the place and the conditions of the migration. These amounts may seem too small to take into account, but we must remember that the income level in the communities is quite low, and in that context the necessary amount of capital becomes an important factor in migrating. In fact, some peasants indicated that they did not migrate during the previous year because they had no money.

How do the peasants finance the capital to migrate? The employer gave an advance to 25% of the migrants; the rest financed themselves or borrowed money in the community. The mechanism of cash advances is an essential part of a specific form of operating the labor market – the *enganche* system, already discussed. The employer usually arrives in the community and gets a commitment from several peasants to work for his enterprise, usually agricultural, in a given time period (for example, in the coffee harvest months), and to formalize the commitment he hands out an advance in cash. We also found cases in which the employer gives money to a peasant returning to his community. The latter then finds more workers and pays them an advance. The *enganche* system applies mainly to agriculture, where labor requirements at specific times of the year are crucial, and the cash advance is the mechanism which assures the provision of that labor.

Although the *enganche* system contributes to the functioning of the labor market in its present stage of development, some peasants feel that it is a system that places them at a disadvantage. One peasant from Acobamba illustrates the problem well when he says: 'The worker who is *enganchado* is jumping into the frying pan. He is paid less than the other workers, and treated badly. The ones who use the system are those who do not have enough money to get to the place of work, and who are not familiar with it. Those in the know take care of their own arrangements, and find good work.' As the labor market in the coastal valleys and eastern *selva* become better developed, the *enganche* system is declining in importance.[4]

The income from temporary migration that has been estimated for this study refers to *net* income, i.e. after deducting from the peasant's monetary wages (including the advance) all the costs incurred in obtaining this income. (As indicated above, these costs consist of transportation, lodging, food, and the costs of obtaining a working capital in order to be able to migrate.) In very few cases was this net income negative. However, many peasants mentioned to us that they did not leave the area to look for work because the cost of transportation, food and lodging has increased considerably in recent years (this being due to the inflationary process that Peru has experienced recently). On the other hand, the wage rates that the peasants received were, in several cases, inferior to those of permanent employees at the same workplace.

Another question included in the survey concerned how the income earned from temporary migrations was utilized. The great majority answered that it was for current expenses, i.e. to increase the amount of monetary income available to buy consumption goods and inputs for agriculture. In a few cases the income was destined for a specific expense, such as fiestas, paying a debt, constructing a house or buying land. While the incursion into the labor market is sometimes brought about by the necessity of some particular expense, it is more than just that. Seasonal migration is fundamentally a regular, stable activity carried out to cover the regular expenses of the family. The peasant's migration is temporary, but the income obtained is part of the family's permanent income. The relationship with the labor market is, in sum, a *social relationship*.

It is principally the adult male who participates in migration. Adult women do migrate, but in very small numbers. The children, on the other hand, migrate in significant proportions. In Ancobamba, 53% of the students surveyed left the community to work during the three months of school vacations (January–March); in Sihuina, this proportion was 33%, and in Huando, 38%. In all these cases the proportion of males who migrated was larger than that of females.

The children who migrate are usually employed in agriculture and services. The children of Huando travel to the Chanchamayo Valley in the *selva* region and to the city of Huancayo; those of Sihuina go to the Quillabamba Valley in the *selva*, and to Cusco. In the cities the children find work as waiters in restaurants, as domestic servants, or as assistants in small shops. The income obtained is usually destined to buy school uniforms and supplies. In this way the children finance part of their own educational costs.

Markets for goods and other markets in the community

A brief review of the functioning of the markets in which the peasants exchange goods will permit us to complete our picture of peasant social relations. The communities of Jacantaya and Culta sell their *A*, *P* and *Z* products principally in the regional fairs of Huancané and Ilave, respectively. Peasants from surrounding communities attend these fairs, which include livestock markets (*q'atu*). There also the peasants make most of their purchases of goods of both urban and rural origin. In both communities shops selling general merchandise are scarce (one in Culta and two in Jacantaya) and small in size.

The communities of Sihuina, Huando and Acobamba are the sites of regional fairs. For this reason, most of these communities' purchases are made in local markets. There are around a dozen general stores in each place, and several are quite large. In none of these communities is there a livestock market, as in the case of Puno's *altiplano* fairs. Animals are sold to merchants who visit the community periodically or to local dealers.

In the three remaining communities (Ttiomayo, Ninamarca and Ancobamba), the goods market is more dispersed. The peasants sell their products to local or outside merchants (called *rescatistas*, or 'ransomers'); they also take things to the regional fair, like those from Ninamarca who go on Sundays to Paucartambo, and those from Ttiomayo who go to Andahuaylillas and Urcos. In addition, there is trade in provincial or departmental capitals: Ninamarca with Cusco and Ancobamba with Abancay, for example. The communities' purchases of goods are also made at different fairs, including the general stores of the community. Only in Ninamarca does no store exist. The purchase of livestock is also done through merchants.

To summarize, there are internal and external markets for the exchange of goods. In the internal market the peasants can sell their *A*, *P* and *Z* products in the local fair, or to merchants who visit the community regularly (and of course also to local 'ransomers'), and they can buy products from the local fair or the shops that exist in the community. In the external market, they can exchange their products in the regional fair in a provincial or departmental capital. Finally, in the livestock market there is a difference between the *altiplano* communities, where the exchange is carried out at fairs, and the other communities, where it is done through local merchants.

Not only goods are exchanged in the peasant communities. As was mentioned earlier, services are exchanged between families in an intensive manner. Apart from labor, there are also markets for land, land rental, and credit. A brief account of these markets is in order.

The land market in the communities is quite limited. The purchase and sale of land is carried out very sporadically, and usually only in cases of emergency. The survey showed very few transactions in the previous three years. With permanent migration of peasant families to cities one would expect significant sales and purchases of land. What we observe, however, is that the migrating families do not sell their lands. Those who leave the community try to leave their lands with relatives and still manage them indirectly. The idea appears to be to hold on to the property in anticipation of any problems that may arise in the city. This economic behavior will be discussed in more detail in the next section. Land rental is another activity which is not very common within the peasant economy. Elderly families tend to rent out their lands when they can no longer work them and there are no children around to take over. In other cases, families who migrate definitively leave their properties under rental. Finally, in some communities there exist plots belonging to the church or municipality which are leased out.

The credit market appears to be more active than the land rental market, although the relevant information was difficult to obtain. Lending money is commonplace. These loans are requested for emergencies, such as illnesses or burials, to pay for a community fiesta, or in order to migrate or carry out a business transaction. Interest is normally not charged directly in cash, but mostly in kind or services. For instance, the borrower may become obligated to help the lender in his plot with two days' work. In many cases credit is obtained in the form of an advance for future work. In this way, the credit market and the labor market become closely related.

Credit for agricultural 'working capital' is less common. This may seem paradoxical if we take into account the credit needs implied by the agricultural process. Nevertheless, there are two reasons for this situation. In the first place, the agricultural process is self-replacing to a great extent, since the farmer himself furnishes inputs such as seeds and labor. In the second place, the necessary 'working capital' is obtained from the gross monetary income which the peasant obtains from different sources, such as the case of temporary migrations which provide income for 'on-farm expenses'.

The logic of exchange in peasant communities: market and personal relations

To summarize, in the peasant economies there is a considerable exchange of productive services between families. There is also an exchange of A, P and Z-goods. For this reason, there exist many forms of exchange (reciprocity, barter, cash) and many goods and services that are exchanged. The majority of goods and services have market prices which are related to the prices in effect in nearby cities or larger external markets.

Nevertheless, there is a characteristic of the transactions which prevents us from speaking of market relationships in an unrestricted way: prices are not always uniform. In many cases the prices vary depending on the persons who trade; in other words, the exchange relationships are not always impersonal. The communities are micro-societies; they are too small for market relationships to eliminate personal relationships entirely and to reach equilibrium market prices.

Market relationships, being impersonal, begin and end with the exchange of commodities in question (including money). There is an immediate, short-term balance. When the relationships are personal, they neither begin nor end with an exchange of a pair of commodities. Thus, there may be an imbalance in the accounts in the short run which will be resolved in the long run. One peasant may rent out his oxen to another peasant at less than the 'market' price now, but later he may request that the latter help him with his harvest when everyone is busy and labor is scarce in the marketplace.

In short, in peasant communities market relationships generally predominate, but they are limited to a certain extent by relationships of a personal nature. This explains the dispersion in the prices (or exchange rates) of the same good in a community. Although the *average* prices in the community follow the changes that occur in the markets which are external to the community, the adjustment process is very slow in the community. This is also due to the existence of personal relations.

Permanent emigrations and returns

In light of the fact that permanent rural–urban migration has been pinpointed as one of the most important social phenomena in Peru during the last decades, we decided to obtain information on this topic in our survey. In particular, we wanted to clear up two issues: first, what proportion of the children emigrate from the community? And secondly, how do they enter into the productive process of the place to which they migrate?

Regarding the first issue, we were able to estimate the total number

Table 6.4 *Residence of the children who left parents' homes (number of persons per family)*

Community	Residence		$\dfrac{(A)}{(A)+(B)} \times 100$
	Emigrated·(A)	Community (B)	
JAC	1.73	0.32	84.4
CUL	1.25	0.53	70.2
ANC	1.50	0.45	76.9
TTI	0.46	0.20	69.7
SIH	1.17	0.34	77.5
HUA	1.26	0.29	81.3
ACO	0.65	0.18	78.3

Note: No data were available for Ninamarca.

of children (both sexes) who have left their parents' houses and then the proportion remaining in the community and the proportion emigrating. Table 6.4 shows the results. The average number of children migrating varies between 0.5 and 1.7 per family, depending on the community. In the southern sierra as a whole there is an average of one child (son or daughter) per family who has emigrated.

The majority of the children who have left their parents' homes have also left the community. Table 6.4 shows that between 70% and 84% of the children no longer living at home have left the community. For the southern sierra the average is close to 75%, i.e. three out of four children emigrated. The figure of 25% (one of every four children remaining in the community) can be taken as a measure of the *retention capacity* of the community as regards the new labor force. From these results we can infer that the problem of scarcity of land (and other resources) in the communities is being resolved through emigration. The low *retention coefficient* is a clear indication that emigration is the peasant economy's answer to the problem of relative overpopulation.[5]

The children who emigrate have one common characteristic in all the communities: they leave at an early age, usually between 15 and 20. A principal motive for migrating so early is to continue studies. This hypothesis is consistent with the fact that in communities with secondary schools, the average age at emigration is higher. Thus Huando has two schools which offer complete primary and secondary levels and an average migrating age of 20. Ancobamba, on the other hand, offers only primary education, and has an average migrating age of 15.

Another fact which supports the hypothesis relating emigration to supply of education is that the educational level of the migrants increases after they leave the community. The average *additional* schooling was found to be between one and two years. There are of course individuals whose educational level remains the same after emigration, even cases of illiterates who do not improve their situation. However, at the other extreme there are persons who left their community with barely any primary education, and who are now studying at the university level.

The current residence of the emigrants is, in the majority of the cases, in Lima or the capital city of a department (Huancayo, Arequipa, Puno, Cusco). There are few cases of emigrants who live in very small cities (such as mining centers), and even fewer migrations to other rural areas. The general pattern is that the children of the peasant family emigrate to large cities. That is the goal. This is shown in Table 6.5.

The occupations of the migrant children are diverse, but with certain identifiable patterns. An important fraction, around a third of

Table 6.5 *Residence and occupation of permanent migrants[a] (number of persons in the sample)*

Occupation	Residence				
	Lima	Large city[b]	Small city[c]	Rural	Total
Wage-earner	26	26	12	8	72
Domestic servant	17	19	2	0	38
Self-employed	10	16	4	0	30
Housewife	11	19	8	0	38
Student	2	7	2	0	11
Other	10	9	2	1	22
Total	76	96	30	9	211

[a] Includes the cases of Jacantaya, Culta, Ancobamba, Huando, Acobamba.
[b] Includes Huancayo, Cusco, Arequipa, Puno.
[c] Includes mining towns.

those who emigrate, are not part of the labor force. These correspond to housewives, students and military personnel. Here we are speaking of *principal* activities, since probably there are many cases of students and housewives who partially participate in income-generating activities.

Of those who are part of the labor force, the majority are wage-earners, as presented in Table 6.5. Only around 20% of the emigrants who work are self-employed (merchants, artisans, street vendors). The majority of the working emigrants, then, enter urban job markets rather than self-employment, as is often claimed. The employment obtained is usually in small enterprises such as repair shops, tailoring, crafts and construction. An important source of employment, especially in the case of women, is as domestic servants. Very few cases were found of emigrants who work in the factories of the modern sector.

The survey included questions concerning returns of any member of the family that had lived for more than a year outside the community (this would give a person 'permanent migrant' status according to our definition). The results appear in Table 6.6. The families who do not have any member who has returned represent various proportions of the total number of families in the community: in Huando only 17% and in Ancobamba half. The sample average suggests that the majority of the families of the sierra have at least one member who has returned after migrating 'permanently'. This result indicates that the linkage of the peasant family with the

Table 6.6 *Returns of members in peasant families (% of families in the sample)*

Community	Members who returned				Average	Standard deviation
	0	1	2	3		
JAC	26.5	29.4	32.4	11.8	1.29	1.00
CUL	37.5	40.0	15.0	7.5	0.93	0.92
ANC	50.0	35.0	15.0	0	0.65	0.74
HUA	16.7	33.3	47.6	2.4	1.36	0.79
ACO	42.5	32.5	25.0	0	0.83	0.81

Note: No data were available for Ninamarca, Ttiomayo or Sihuina.

rest of the Peruvian economy is quite diverse; it also indicates that the peasant family's experience with the outside world goes beyond the relations of exchange of goods and labor during the year. In the same way, its degree of integration is greater than that which results from measuring only annual monetary income.

The reasons for returning to the community are various, but some patterns are recognizable. Of 110 cases of return for which we have information, we observe in Table 6.7 that half were due to problems related to the parents of the emigrant, whether they died, fell ill, became invalids or were very old. This is the case when there are no more children in the community who can help the parents or take charge of the land and other resources. The other important cause of the migrants' return is work. Of the 110 who went back to the community, 22 did so because they lost their job, had a low income, or could not adjust to the work (principally the case of those working in mining). There was also a significant number of returns (14) due to illness. Finally, there were 14 cases of return due to problems with the landholdings which the emigrants had left in the community. The problems include those arising from litigation, squatters and the agrarian reform.

Although the data in Table 6.7 are not sufficiently statistically significant to study the problem of returns and arrive at more solid conclusions at the regional level, they do give an indication of certain behavior patterns in the peasant family. The cases of return due to

Table 6.7 *Reasons for returning (number of persons in the sample)*

Reasons	Communities					
	JAC	CUL	ANC	HUA	ACO	Total
1. Losing the job	3	2	0	1	3	9
2. Low income	2	0	2	0	0	4
3. Maladaptation	0	0	3	4	2	9
4. Sickness	3	0	0	10	1	14
5. Problems with land	2	1	6	4	1	14
6. Problems with parents	22	12	7	11	2	54
7. Others	4	2	0	0	0	6
Total	36	17	18	30	9	110

work problems or illness (cases 1–4) require that the migrant have a place to which to return, i.e. that he has his land reserved in some way. In effect, many declarations of the peasants, as well as personal observations in the communities, indicate with some certainty that the migrant does not divorce himself from his plot of land. He does not 'burn his bridges' upon leaving. As was indicated in the previous section, there is no land market which emerges from emigration. The parcel of land thus comprises an income safeguard for the family who emigrates. One can always return to the farm. Thus, during the period of the survey, some individuals were returning to the community because of the current economic crisis in Peru, which is more severe in the cities.

Reasons 5 and 6 reflect behavior complementary to that of maintaining one's lands in reserve. Here the issue is not losing title to the parcel. The death or incapacity of the parents endangers the possession of the land on the part of the family or heirs. There are many legal actions in the communities stemming from land, and one way of avoiding these problems is for a son or a daughter to be present. In several cases we found persons who had returned as a result of pressure from other children of the family who could not go back to the farm so easily. Someone had to return to take care of the land, animals and buildings; if not, someone else might take it all away. The reasons for a migrant returning to resolve problems relating to his own land are even more obvious.

In the reasons for returning we may, in consequence, recognize a certain strategy in the economic behavior of the peasant. He maintains links with the community, where he has a 'reserve' consisting of his or his parents' lands, and to which he can return if he meets failure in the outside world. The strategy of the family is thus to avoid the risk of losing the land.[6] The phenomenon of emigrations is usually seen as a flow of people in one direction, from the countryside to the city. The evidence presented here shows that there is an important feedback in terms of individuals returning from the city to the country. Emigrations and returns are movements guided by the economic strategy of the peasant family.

7

Stagnation in the peasant economy and the role of demand

The previous chapters have shown production and exchange structures in today's peasant communities in Peru. The peasant economy was observed at a given point in time (1978–9). This chapter will attempt to depict the dynamic of the peasant economy in Peru in the recent decades. If this is an economy very much integrated to the market system, has economic growth experienced in the Peruvian economy reached the peasantry? Have rapid population growth and urbanization induced growth in peasants' income through higher levels of demand for food?

Growth and distribution in Peru: 1948–75

The income distribution problem presents peculiar characteristics in the underdeveloped countries. It not only refers to the problem of inequality, but also includes the problem of absolute poverty. For this reason, in order to evaluate the performance of an underdeveloped economy in terms of the distributive problem, it is necessary to determine the changes which have occurred both in the degree of inequality as well as in the proportion of the population still living in conditions of absolute poverty.

In the last three decades, Peru has experienced various patterns of economic growth, initially based in export of primary products, followed by import substitution industrialization. Also, it has undergone periods of both rapid growth and recession. On the other hand, Peru passed through diverse socio-political contexts. From the initiation of the government of General Odria in 1948 until 1968, economic policy was basically liberal. Certainly one can draw distinctions concerning the degree of liberalism manifested: it was much more marked in the Odria and Prado regimes; there was a greater degree of State intervention in the first Belaunde government.

However, overall, the economy in this period (1948–68) can be characterized as 'free enterprise' or *laissez-faire*, wherein the role of the State in the productive process was very limited.

The military regime of Velasco (1968–75) was characterized, in the economic domain, by three traits: a reform program treating land and capital property; a growth program based even more strongly in import substitution industrialization; and a greater State role in economic activity, particularly via the formation of public enterprises. The Morales period (1975–80), the 'second phase' of the military government, constituted a period substantially different from that of Velasco. There were neither reform programs nor growth strategies. The economic crisis became the central economic problem and governmental action centered itself around stabilization policies. The second Belaunde government, inaugurated in July 1980, denotes a return to liberalism on the part of the State.

The period of economic liberalism: 1948–68

From the immediate post-war era until the final years of the 1960s, Peru experienced rapid economic growth with price stability. This is depicted in Table 7.1. The real per capita income increased at an average annual rate of 2.5% and the average annual inflation rate was 8%. The growth pattern during the Odria and Prado regimes was based in primary product export, fundamentally of agricultural, mining and fishing products. Economic policy was directed principally toward providing incentives for these exports. Economic growth was led by the export sector.[1] The industrial growth observed in those years was more the result of its technological link to processing and support of exports (Thorp and Bertram, 1978). Nevertheless, after the first Belaunde government there began a change in the growth pattern, toward one based in import substitution industrialization. This change can be seen in Table 7.1, comparing the relative stagnation of exports and the relative growth of the manufacturing sector in the first Belaunde regime.

In order to analyze the distribution problem in Peru, it is necessary to distinguish three sectors in the productive structure. The large, modern firms (whether urban or rural) constitute the so-called 'modern sector', and in them capitalist relations of production are predominant. The 'urban traditional sector' and the 'rural traditional sector' are composed of the rest of the workers in each area. In these latter two sectors the small firm and the family economic unit are the

Table 7.1 *Peru: growth, inflation, distribution and pattern of growth, 1950–80 (annual rates and %)*

	Odria 1950–6	Prado 1957–62	Belaunde 1963–8	Velasco 1969–75	Morales 1976–80
Growth					
Real GNP per capita	3.7	2.9	1.1	2.9	−1.5
Inflation					
CPI – Lima	6.6	8.0	12.8	10.7	51.3
Growth pattern					
Exports/GNP	15.6	21.2	21.0	16.0	14.8
Manufactures/GNP	14.0	16.5	18.8	20.5	20.6
Distribution					
Profits/Nat. income	15.5	13.3	16.1	20.1	28.4
Growth in average real income of workers					
Modern sector		3.4		3.0	−5.8
Urban traditional		1.7		1.2	−2.2
Rural traditional		0.9		1.0	−2.0

Source: See Appendix IV.

predominant forms of organization of production. About 1961, the 'modern sector', empirically defined as firms with more than five workers, employed 20% of the workforce; in the 'urban traditional sector' were 30%; in the 'rural traditional sector' were 50% (Webb, 1977). By far the largest social group in the 'traditional rural sector' was constituted by peasant families living in the sierra. Given this economic structure, four income categories appear appropriate for the study of the income distribution process in Peru: profits and wages in the 'modern sector' and incomes in the urban and rural 'traditional' sectors, which are composed mainly of wages and income from self-employment.

Webb (1977) demonstrated that toward the beginning of the 1960s the composition of the income pyramid was the following: the top 1% was composed of owners of the means of production and of professionals; the next stratum comprised high-level employees in the 'modern sector'. These groups constitute what may be called the

Peruvian 'middle class', which is approximately 5% of the population.[2] The rest of the highest quartile consisted of workers and employees of the 'modern sector'. The relatively privileged position of these wage and salary earners is a consequence of the fact that the owners of the means of production, together with the 'middle class', constitute a very small group in Peru and this does not signify that they have a high level of living. The workers of the 'urban traditional sector' are located in the following stratum in the income pyramid. Together the above groups constitute the upper half of the income pyramid. In the lower half we mainly encounter peasant families. The lowest 30% was constituted almost exclusively by peasants who live in the sierra.

An estimate of income trends for these groups during the period 1950–66 was also made by Webb. His results indicate that the average real income of the 'modern sector' increased by 4% annually; that of the 'urban traditional sector' increased by 2% annually and that of the 'rural traditional sector' increased by only 1% annually; while the peasants of the sierra experienced practically no gain in real income during this period (Webb, 1977: Table 3.7). On the other hand, the average profit income of owner-families increased in a greater proportion than did the average income in the nation.[3] Therefore, during the liberal period the process of economic growth mainly benefitted the upper quartile of the income distribution. The group which benefitted least consisted of the neediest families.

Congruent with the liberal economic context, the most important redistributive policy during the period was conducted via the government budget. In fact, the budget as a proportion of the GNP grew from 12–13% in 1950 to 17–18% in 1968 (Banco Central de Reserva, *Cuentas Nacionales*). Nevertheless, as Webb also demonstrated, the *net* result of the transfers via the government budget was moderately progressive. Despite the fact that greater tax receipts came from the 'modern sector', the greater part of government expenditure also went to families of this sector. Income redistribution did not change the results of the market.

The period of reforms: 1968–75

The Revolutionary Government of the Armed Forces initiated in 1968 a series of reforms, the intent of which was to alter the structures of Peruvian society. One of the objectives of the military regime was to carry through a radical policy of income redistribution. Given the degree of inequality which exists in Peru, income redistribution is clearly a policy which benefits those at the base of the income pyramid. The empirical basis for this assertion arises from Webb's study: a selective transfer of 5% of the national income, taken from the upper 1% and given to the lower tercile of the population, would reduce the absolute income of the former group by only 16%, but it would *double* the incomes of the latter group. In contrast, a very successful economic growth effort consisting of a sustained growth rate of 3% annually would require more than 20 years to achieve the same improvement in the income of the lowest tercile (as the hypothetical redistribution discussed above). Therefore, and contrary to the belief held by many, to redistribute income in a selective manner in Peru does not imply a redistribution of poverty.

The most important reforms having a direct impact on the redistribution of income were the sectoral reforms. In the mining, fishing and industrial sectors these reforms consisted of giving workers the right to participate in profits, ownership and management of the enterprises. The reforms created 'Labor Communities' (*Comunidades Laborales*) formed by workers from each firm, with the right to participate in the profits of the firms in the following proportions: 25% for industry, 20% for fishing and 10% for mining. Approximately one-third of the participation was distributed in the form of income and the balance was provided as an acquisition of the firm's patrimony in the name of the respective 'Labor Community'. The enterprises affected by the reform were those of the 'modern sector' and its beneficiaries, the workers of this sector. The latter group, as was indicated above, belongs to the richest quartile.

The Agrarian Reform Law, promulgated in 1969, sought to redistribute land ownership, eliminating indirect forms of agrarian exploitation so that the 'land belongs to those who work it'. The affected lands were to benefit: (1) workers organized in cooperatives; (2) peasant communities; (3) individuals; (4) a special economic entity, called SAIS, which is a mixture of cooperative and peasant communities. The initial goals of the reform, both in terms of number of persons as well as of quantity of land affected, were practically achieved by the end of 1979. The reform transferred approximately 40% of total land area to 360,000 families (Caballero and Alvarez, 1980: Tables 1 and 6). These beneficiaries represent around 25% of all the rural families in the country.

Who were the beneficiaries of the Agrarian Reform? In terms of families, 27% were ex-wage-earners, the majority of whom were located in the modern farms on the coast; 25% were ex-workers of the hacienda system, the majority of whom were located in the sierra; 38% were peasant families who lived in peasant communities; the balance (10%) were 'individual' families (Caballero and Alvarez, 1980: Table 6). But these percentages do not reflect the real reassignment of lands between families due to the difference in the size of the lands assigned to each group. The study by Caballero and Alvarez demonstrates that in the case of peasant families the average land size adjudicated per family is one-fifth of the total's average adjudication (ibid.). Thus, the income transfer to peasant families was very small: the reform reached only 14% of all peasant families and even for this 14% the quantity transferred per family was much lower than the average per family transfer given to other groups. Actually, those who most benefitted were the ex-wage-earners of the large farms on the coast which belonged to the 'modern sector' and, for this reason, to the richest quartile in the income pyramid.

The redistributive effect of all the sectoral reforms was the transfer of around 2% or 3% of national income from the upper percentile to approximately 18% of the labor force (Figueroa, 1975). This income transfer took place almost completely within the richest quartile. The reason is simple: the reforms were concentrated basically in the 'modern sector' of each of the sectors involved. The redistribution of income within the 'modern sector' – characterized by extreme heterogeneity in productivity levels among firms – was biased against the 'traditional sector'. The great majority of workers in the latter sector, that is, the poorest groups, were left outside the design of the reforms. The formation of public enterprises, on the other hand, constituted a restructuring of ownership in the 'modern sector', without significantly affecting the capitalist rules of production and distribution in the economy (Baer and Figueroa, 1981).

The overall Peruvian economic performance during the reform period was similar to the liberal period as much in terms of economic growth as in price stability. The average growth rate of per capita real income was 2.9% annually and the inflation rate was 11% annually, as shown in Table 7.1. As for the growth pattern, in this period significant emphasis was placed on industrial growth via import substitution. The industrial policy was excessively protectionist, not only because of the high tariffs but also because of the almost massive prohibitions on industrial good imports which competed with those produced domestically.

As a result of the economic growth, of the change in the pattern of growth and the redistribution of income via the sectoral reforms, the nature of income inequality showed at the same time change and continuity with respect to the liberal period. The element of continuity was that the growth of average worker income in the three sectors was differentiated: in the 'modern sector' it grew at a greater rate than the 'traditional sectors', as shown in Table 7.1. In this sense, inequality between workers increased. The element of change was that the participation in firms' profits increased in the national income: from 15–16%, it passed to 20%. Paradoxically, in the period of reforms and greater state interventionism, the share of profits in national income increased. Surely, one reason for this increase can be found in the development pattern based on excessive industrial protectionism.

Capitalist development and rural incomes: nature of the problem

The result that peasants' real incomes have remained almost stagnant in the period 1950–75 challenges the common view that economic growth in the capitalist modern sector can induce an overall increase in real incomes in the non-capitalist system of the economy. The explanation for this failure of the capitalist development in Peru cannot rely on the hypothesis of 'dualism'. Stagnation in the real income of peasants is not due to the lack of integration into the capitalist economy. This study has shown that the peasant economy is very well integrated into the market system. The outcome must be explained in terms of the working of the market system and the effects of economic policies.

On the other hand, the outcome of the land reform program indicates that exploitation of peasants through non-capitalist relations, that is, through non-wage relations, is not of great importance. Land reform was directed to the elimination of feudal-type relations on the sierra and only 10% of the peasantry was part of the program. Peasants are connected to the rest of the economy basically through market relations.

Why is it that capitalist development has not generated overall development – in particular, improvements in the standard of living of the peasantry?

One of the main features of economic development in Peru and in Latin America is the continuous decline in agricultural output to total output. The share of agriculture in the Gross National Product of the region has declined by almost a half in 35 years: from 25% in 1940 to 12% in 1975 (UN–CEPAL, 1978). In the case of Peru these ratios declined from 23% in 1950 to 12% in 1980 (Peru, Banco Central, 1968, 1981). The decline of the share of agriculture in GNP is not an economic problem *per se*. Actually this change in the production structure has also taken place in the developed countries. However, what is specific to the present Latin American historical stage is the fact that the relative decline in agriculture is associated with the prevalence of rural poverty. In Latin America poverty is concentrated basically in the rural areas.[4] Thus, a change in the share of agriculture in national income has direct implications for income distribution and, even more importantly, for absolute poverty.

The usual explanation for the decline in the share of agriculture is that income elasticities for food consumption are very low. This is the well-known Engel's law of food expenditure. In the case of Peru and Latin America, however, a rapid increase in population is taking place which must have a bearing on the demand for food. Given the same average income, expenditure for food must increase at the same rate as population growth. To this 'population-effect', we should add the 'income-effect' due to the increase in average income brought about by the economic development process. Engel's law will apply to the second effect, whereas the 'population-effect' will be shifting the Engel curve upward through time. The figures presented for Peru in the period 1950–74 indicate a rate of growth of approximately 5% per year in food expenditure in real terms. This is a result of using 2.8% for population growth and 2.5% for per capita real income as annual growth rates, and 0.7 as the income elasticity.[5] However, the actual average growth rate of agriculture has been only 2.8% for the same period.

The other feature in the process of development in Peru (and in Latin America) is the rapid urbanization process. Although the total demand for food may not be greatly affected by changes in the urban–rural distribution of population, these changes will increase the links between the city and the countryside stemming from food consumption. Moreover, with rapid urbanization, per capita income in the rural sector should be increasing rapidly as more people will be spending on food and relatively fewer people will be producing it. If we consider again the figure for Peru of 5% as the 'theoretical' agriculture output growth rate and take 1% as the growth rate in rural population, per capita real income should be growing at a rate of 4% in rural areas. Clearly this is not happening in Peru, at least as a long-run trend.

The two characteristics of development in Peru – population growth and urbanization – lead us to expect a much more dynamic agriculture than is suggested by the income elasticity explanation. Yet, we observe a rather slowly growing agriculture. This result must come either from a change in consumption patterns – that is, shifts in *aggregate* Engel curves for food expenditure – or from a change in the production structure of the economy due to changes in the international division of labor, because in open economies agricultural output depends not only on domestic consumption patterns but on patterns of specialization in international trade as well. Alternatively, the rate of growth may be due to a combination of both effects. In order to analyze these effects a theoretical model is developed in the next section.

A model of derived demand for rural factors

Given the rapid increase in urban population and also in average urban income in Latin America, it is clear that the demand for food comes mainly from the cities. In this section, a simple model is constructed in order to determine the relationship between urban and rural incomes derived from the urban consumption of food. The income generated in the rural sector due to food expenditure in the cities will be called the 'derived rural income'. The economy will be divided into three productive sectors: two food-producing sectors, agriculture and the food-processing industry, and all remaining sectors which will be called 'rest'. There are three types of food: the two corresponding to the domestic sectors mentioned above and imported food. The productive sectors are inter-related, as shown in Table 7.2, which can be seen as an input–output table of the Leontief type.

The total rural income (or value added) generated, directly and indirectly, by a unit of final demand in each sector will require to take into account all the inter-relations of Table 7.2. Solving for all the 'rounds' involved in the process of production, we get:

$$VA_1 = a_{01}[A_{11}(C_1^* + D_1) + A_{12}(C_2^* + D_2) + A_{13}D_3] \qquad (1)$$

where a_{01} is the direct coefficient of value added per unit of gross sale

Table 7.2 *Input–output table for food production–consumption analysis*

	Agri-culture	Food process	'Rest'	Final demand Food consump.	Others	Total
Agriculture	X_{11}	X_{12}	X_{13}	C_1^*	D_1	X_1
Food processing	X_{21}	X_{22}	X_{23}	C_2^*	D_2	X_2
'Rest'	X_{31}	X_{32}	X_{33}	0	D_3	X_3
Imports: food	X_{ml}	X_{m2}	X_{m3}	C_m^*	0	X_m
Imports: others	X_{nl}	X_{n2}	X_{n3}	0	D_n	X_n
Value added	VA_1	VA_2	VA_3			
Total gross value	X_1	X_2	X_3			

in agriculture; the $A_{1j}s$ are the coefficients of direct and indirect requirements of commodity 1 to produce one unit of final product of sector j, which come from the solution of the Leontief system. From equation (1) we derive total coefficients of value added as:

$$VA_1 = B_{01}(C_1^* + D_1) + B_{02}(C_2^* + D_2) + B_{03}D_3 \qquad (2)$$

where $B_{0j} \equiv a_{01}A_{1j}$. Thus, B_{01} measures the amount of increase in agriculture income due to an increase in one unit of food consumption of type 1, that is agricultural food; B_{02} measures the same effect for the case of processed food. Coefficient B_{03} does not concern us here because it is connected to non-food consumption. We shall assume here that imports and exports are independent, so there will be no rural income generated from consumption of imported food (C_m^*).

The consumption expenditures in the three types of food can be written as follows:

$$C_u = C_1 + C_2 + C_m \qquad (3)$$

where C_1 stands for the expenditure on agricultural food, C_2 for processed food, and C_m for imported food. Since this is the value of family expenditure in the city, not all this expenditure goes to the rural sector. In Table 7.2, values are at producers' prices (C_i^*) but in equation (3) they are at consumers' prices (C_i). The difference between the price the producer gets and the price the consumer pays, usually called 'trade margins', will be assumed to be a fixed amount for each type of food: t_1, t_2. Therefore, the amount of expenditure going to the rural sector would be:

$$C^* = (1 - t_1)C_1 + (1 - t_2)C_2 \qquad (4)$$
$$= C_1^* + C_2^*$$

where C_i^* corresponds to the consumption column of Table 7.2.

From equation (2) we know that for each unit of sales of agricultural goods, rural income increases by B_{01}, and by B_{02} in the case of processed food. Then, *total* rural income (I_{ur}) derived from an urban family expenditure on food will be:

$$I_{ur} = B_{01}C_1^* + B_{02}C_2^*$$
$$= B_{01}(1 - t_1)C_1 + B_{02}(1 - t_2)C_2 \qquad (5)$$

If we represent equation (5) as a ratio of the family's income (I_u), we will get the 'derived rural income' ratio:

$$\frac{I_{ur}}{I_u} = B_{01}(1 - t_1)\frac{C_1}{I_u} + B_{02}(1 - t_2)\frac{C_2}{I_u}$$
$$= \frac{C_u}{I_u}\left[B_{01}(1 - t_1)\frac{C_1}{C_u} + B_{02}(1 - t_2)\frac{C_2}{C_u} \right] \qquad (6)$$

This ratio is a measure of the income generated in the rural sector due to the urban family's food expenditure. It is the rural income content of the urban family's expenditure. The higher the value of this ratio, the stronger the connection between urban–rural incomes.

Figure 7.1 summarizes the relations established in the model. The vertical axis measures expenditure and the horizontal axis income. The Engel curve for food expenditure is labeled E. From this curve we derive the proportion of the expenditure which becomes rural income. Curve R shows this 'derived rural income', which also varies with the level of family income. The 'derived rural income' ratio is just the proportion of income that is spent on rural factors of production, e.g. AN/OA, when family income is OA, in Figure 7.1.

Let us call α the ratio of 'derived rural income' with respect to average family income in the city ($\bar{I}_u$). Thus:

$$I_{ur} = \alpha\bar{I}_u \qquad (7)$$

'Total derived rural income' represented by Y_{ur} as a proportion of total urban income (Y_u) will also be equal to α. The other ratio of

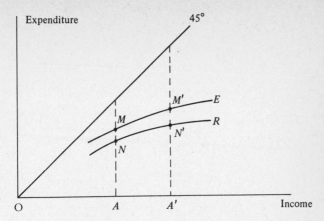

Figure 7.1 Engel curve and derived rural income curve

interest is the 'total derived rural income' per head in the rural sector. Let us call N_u and N_r the populations of the urban and rural sectors, respectively. Then:

$$\frac{Y_{ur}}{N_r} = \frac{I_{ur}N_u}{N_r} = \alpha \bar{I}_u \left(\frac{N_u}{N_r}\right) \tag{8}$$

Equation (8) says that the per capita income generated in the rural sector by the urban expenditure on food depends on three factors: the 'derived rural income ratio', the average urban income, and the ratio of urban population to rural population. These last two factors are increasing rapidly in Peru and therefore rural per capita income should be increasing fast. However, α reduces the effect of those factors because it decreases as average income goes up. We need to know more about the determinants of α and its tendencies in order to assess the combined effect of the three variables on the growth of rural incomes.

As shown by equation (6), the 'derived rural income' ratio depends on four sets of coefficients: the average propensity to spend on food, trade margins, production structure, and the mix of types of food consumed. In the next section, an estimate of these coefficients will be made for the case of Peru. This will provide us with an application of the model as we will estimate empirically curves E and R shown in Figure 7.1.

An empirical estimate for 1970

The availability of an input–output table for Peru and a family budget study for its largest city (Lima) for the same period (1969–70) will enable us to make an empirical estimate of equation (6). The input–output table has been rearranged according to the sectors defined in the model. The relevant segment of the rearranged table is presented in Table 7.3. The direct coefficients computed from this table are:

$$a_0 = 0.7170$$
$$a_{11} = 0.1896 \qquad a_{21} = 0.0522$$
$$a_{12} = 0.1626 \qquad a_{22} = 0.1246$$

The corresponding B_{0j} coefficients of equation (2) are:

$$VA_1 = 0.8940C_1^* + 0.1635C_2^* \qquad (9)$$

Thus, for each *sol* of sale of agricultural food, 0.89 becomes rural income; whereas for processed food this becomes only 0.16.

The family budget data for Lima comes from a study carried out within the ECIEL Program. The structure of family spending by income quartiles is presented in Table 7.4. Families in the lowest quartile spend 54% of their budget on food, whereas in the richest quartile this proportion declines to 31%. The average expenditure ratio in Lima is 43%.

In spite of the recurrent discussion on the issue of trade margins, there are no systematic studies in Peru showing the magnitudes involved. Here we have made some gross estimates based on

Table 7.3 *Peru: production structure for food, 1969 (producer's price, billions of soles)*

	Agriculture	Processing	Consumption
Agriculture	6.9	4.7	21.8
Food processing	1.9	3.5	19.2
Rest	1.0	5.6	0
Imported inputs	0.5	4.2	1.5
Value added	26.1	10.9	
Total gross value	36.4	28.9	

Source: Instituto Nacional de Planificación (1973).

Table 7.4 *Lima: structure of family spending, 1969 (%)*

	Quartiles				
Item	I	II	III	IV	Total
Food	54	47	41	31	43
Housing	16	17	21	26	20
Durables	8	10	9	12	9
Clothing	7	7	9	8	8
Transportation	3	6	4	6	5
Others	12	13	16	17	15
Total	100	100	100	100	100
Average expenditure	49	61	100	191	100
Derived rural income ratio[a]	19	17	15	11	15

[a] See text for the methodology used in these estimates.
Source: Figueroa (1974: Table 9).

fragmentary information on particular goods and also on the data contained in the original input–output table for Peru. For agricultural goods, the coefficient of trade margins has been estimated at 33% and for processed food at 20%.[6]

Regarding the mix in which the three types of food are consumed, we will assume that all families consume them in the same proportion. There are no data available on these proportions. This assumption leads to an overestimation of processed food and imported food as a proportion of total food expenditure for low-income families, which should not be exaggerated, however. An important proportion of 'popular food' in Peru is imported and/or processed, such as noodles, bread, oil and fats, milk and sugar. The proportions to be used as estimates will accordingly be those appearing in the last column of Table 7.3: agricultural food 51%, processed food 45% and imported food 4%.

To summarize, the estimates that have been made so far are:

$$t_1 = 0.33 \qquad B_{01} = 0.89 \qquad C_1/C = 0.51$$
$$t_2 = 0.20 \qquad B_{02} = 0.16 \qquad C_2/C = 0.45$$

As these coefficients are independent of the income bracket of the family, the 'derived rural income' for families in different quartiles will vary according to the average propensity to spend on food. Thus for the lowest quartile of Lima we have:

$$\frac{I_r}{I_u} = 0.54\{0.66 \times 0.89 \times 0.51 + 0.80 \times 0.16 \times 0.45\}$$
$$= 0.19$$

Hence, the poorest quartile of Lima spends 19% of their family budget on rural factors of production. This proportion for each income quartile is shown at the bottom of Table 7.4. The average coefficient for Lima turns out to be 0.15, which means that only 15% of Lima's total income goes to the countryside as rural income as a consequence of food consumption. In sum, the first row of this table shows the empirical Engel curve and the last row the 'derived rural income' ratio. These are the empirical counterparts of curves E and R presented in Figure 7.1 in terms of ratios.

This empirical result shows, first, that the 'derived rural income' ratio is relatively low. *The average proportion of family budget spent on food is 43% in Lima, yet only 15% becomes rural income.* If OA were average income in Figure 7.1, NA would be a third of MA in the case of Lima. Secondly, the 'derived rural income' ratio declines as family income rises. Our estimation procedures have led us to a constant vertical distance between the Engel curve and the 'derived rural income curve', which need not be the case if the consumption mix of different types of food varies with income.[7]

'Derived rural income' trends and income concentration

The main purpose of this and the next section is to present some hypotheses to explain the slow growth of rural income in Latin America. One coordinate in the analysis is the intensity in the derived demand for rural factors of production. For the case of domestic demand for food we have developed a simple model to relate urban incomes and expenditures to rural incomes (export demand will be discussed in the next section). The model was summarized in equation (8). From that equation, we can advance some hypotheses on the possible trends of the relevant variables involved so as to estimate changes in the 'derived rural income'.

It is clear from equation (8) that, other things being equal, a process of urbanization increases the intensity of demand for rural factors.

More people of equal average income in the cities will be generating a higher 'derived rural income' which in per capita terms will increase even more because of the rural population's relative stagnation. If for each family in the countryside there is a family in the city, this family will be generating income in the amount $\alpha \bar{I}_u$ for his fellow *campesino*; however, if there is now a process of urbanization by which for each family in the countryside there are two families in the city, income accruing to those rural families will double.

To this 'urbanization effect' we must add the 'pure income effect' due to the increase in the average income $(\bar{I}_u)$ in Latin American cities, which is brought about by the economic growth process in the economy. That increase will augment income for the rural people but not proportionally, due to Engel's law; that is, the α ratio will decline. The question is, however, whether α will decline due only to Engel's law, or whether other variables affected by the particular process of economic growth could also change α.

Let the curves E and R in Figure 7.1 represent the aggregation of all individual curves, so that the axes now measure average income and expenditures. For the E-curve to represent a given pattern of consumption income distribution must be held constant along the curve, only in this case the elasticity of the aggregate Engel curve will have the same value as the individual Engel curve. The 'pure' Engel's law will then apply to a given pattern of consumption, that is to an E-curve where income distribution is held constant. Therefore, changes in income distribution will cause a shift in the aggregate Engel curve. The economic growth process in Peru has, as shown above, been accompanied by a higher concentration of income. The effect of the more unequal income distribution is a downward shift in the E-curve, which in turn will shift downwards the R-curve. This result comes from differences in average and marginal propensities to spend on food between income groups.

The other effect of higher income concentration upon the 'derived rural income' comes from differences in the mix of types of food between income groups. It is expected that marginal propensities to spend on imported food are higher for the rich. The same can be said about processed food.[8] Given the lower content of rural factors in these latter types of food, as illustrated above, the effect is to shift the R-curve downward. *One implication of the higher concentration of income in Latin America is, therefore, a further decrease in the 'derived rural income'.*

The effect of change in patterns of international trade

In open economies, agricultural output depends not only on domestic consumption patterns but also on patterns of specialization in international trade. Therefore, if domestic patterns of food consumption have not created enough stimulus for higher rural incomes, there exists the alternative that foreign demand might have. After all, the international division of labor has usually been presented as that of developed countries producing manufactures and less developed countries producing agricultural products. The fact is, however, that foreign demand for agricultural commodities produced in Peru has not been dynamic. The share of agriculture in total exports from Peru has declined from 55% in 1950 to 20% in 1974 (Banco Central, 1968 and 1976). On the imports side, Table 7.5 shows an increase in the proportion of food imports to total production for the basic foodstuffs between 1943 and 1975.

The changes in the structure of exports and imports in Peru are certainly a reflection of changes that have been taking place in the international division of labor, particularly after World War II. First, in this period world exports have grown faster than GNP in both developed and underdeveloped countries, which means that the world as a whole has seen its degree of integration increased. However, export growth is faster in developed countries (Donges, 1979). Secondly, in terms of exports of agricultural commodities, the developed countries' share has increased from 49% in 1955 to 61% in 1975, whereas the share of the developing countries has decreased from 40% to 26%. Currently, the United States supplies 60% of

Table 7.5 *Peru: imports/domestic output ratios for basic imported food (%)*

	1943	1960	1965	1970	1975
Wheat	49	70	76	84	86
Corn	n.a.	n.a.	0	1	52
Oilfats	4	35	34	80	80
Milk	3	22	22	35	41
Beef	2	4	12	28	11
Rice	10	10	32	0	12
Barley	2	6	10	10	32

Source: Lajo (1979).

grains sold in the international market. The less developed countries, as Donges points out, 'have lost ground in fields where their resource endowments should have given them a comparative advantage: in food products, agricultural raw materials...' (p. 11). Thirdly, exports of manufactures from the underdeveloped countries are increasing their share in world trade. These changes in patterns of trade can be seen in Table 7.6.

An explanation for the change in the comparative advantage in agricultural products lies in the tremendous increase in agricultural productivity in developed countries. Agricultural economists have argued that this increased productivity is due to a change from resource-based agriculture to science-based agriculture. Hayami and Ruttan (1971), for instance, have reported the fact that for several products agricultural productivity differences between the developed and less developed countries have widened. They conclude: 'The basis for comparative advantage shifted from natural resource endowments to the endowments of scientific and industrial capacity. The shift in comparative advantage in agricultural production from the less developed to the developed countries was accelerated after World War II' (p. 242). As a result of this technological change, land has increased in terms of efficiency-units in developed countries which have become relatively land-abundant.

In addition to this shift in natural comparative advantage, economic policies have pushed relative prices in the same direction: developed countries protect agriculture whereas less developed countries protect manufacturing. Agricultural prices supports, tariffs and quotas on imports are clear cases of the former. In less developed countries policies for import substitution industrialization have led to a decrease in agricultural relative prices.

All these shifts in comparative advantage (natural and induced by economic policies) have resulted in a change in international trade patterns. The significant decline in the share of agriculture in total exports, together with the fact that the share of imported food has increased with respect to total agricultural output, indicate that Peru has, in fact, lost comparative advantage in agriculture. Mostly, agriculture in Peru is still based on natural resource endowments.

A consequence of this shift in the international trade pattern for agricultural development in Peru is that the production structure of the national economy shifts away from agriculture. The *level* of agricultural output decreases relatively. This is the result of the slow

Table 7.6 Changes in world export structure (%)

	SITC	Developed countries			Developing countries[a]					
					Total			Excluding OPEC		
		1955	1970	1975	1955	1970	1975	1955	1970	1975
Food and related products	0 + 1 + 22 + 4	48.7	59.0	63.3	42.6	31.8	28.7	41.0	29.3	27.5
Agricultural raw materials	2 excluding 22, 27, 28	49.4	58.4	61.3	40.4	30.3	26.2	38.5	25.6	24.3
Crude fertilizers and minerals	27 + 28	52.6	58.0	54.3	33.0	31.4	32.8	31.5	28.0	29.7
Mineral fuels	3	31.7	26.5	17.4	57.5	63.1	73.9	9.0	10.1	11.0
Chemical products	5	88.1	88.9	87.3	5.1	3.9	5.4	5.0	3.7	4.6
Machinery and transport equipment	7	86.6	87.6	87.1	0.7	1.6	2.8	0.6	1.5	2.7
Iron and steel	67	86.6	82.5	86.5	0.9	3.3	2.7	0.9	3.1	2.5
Non-ferrous metals and products	68	59.2	63.6	67.9	33.9	29.0	22.0	33.5	28.6	21.2
Other manufactures	6 + 8 excluding 67, 68	82.6	79.9	78.1	8.8	11.2	13.4	8.7	10.9	13.0
Total export	0–9	64.7	71.9	66.2	25.4	17.6	24.1	22.5	11.8	11.4

[a] Excluding centrally planned economies.

Source: UNCTAD, Handbook of International Trade and Development statistics, 1976; UN, Monthly Bulletin of Statistics, May 1977. Taken from Donges (1979), p. 12.

growth in exports and, on the domestic demand side, the increase in the ratio of imports to total production. An increase in this ratio shifts the R-curve further down because a shift in this curve also comes from a process of saving rural factors of production, that is by reducing the B_{0j} coefficients of equation (6). It is an import substitution process in reverse.

Another effect to be examined is on the *structure* of the agricultural production. The question is, what has happened to the growth of output in the peasant economy? A study made by Hopkins (1981) shows that in the period 1944–69 agricultural output in Peru grew at the average rate of 2.8% per year, but output produced basically in the peasant economy of the sierra grew only by 0.5%. The situation in the first half of the 1970s must have been very similar.[9] Total agricultural output grew at similar rates and no change of significance was observed in the peasant economy to expect a different growth rate in its output.

In conclusion, in the period 1950–75 there was a change in the level and in the structure of the agricultural production in Peru. The relative stagnation was more severe in the peasant economy's output. This change in production structure implies that the peasant economy plays a less important role as supplier of food for domestic consumption over time. Food supply for urban markets comes increasingly from the medium- and large-sized farms and, above all, from imports.

8

Economic crisis and the peasant economy, 1975–1980

The second half of the 1970s has been a period of economic crisis in Peru. The real GNP per capita of 1980 is almost 10% less than that of 1974. The annual rate of inflation has varied between 24% and 70%. Neither the decrease in real average income, nor the rates of inflation, nor the duration of the crisis has any parallel in the recent economic history of Peru. Since 1950 two short periods of crisis are recorded (1957–9 and 1967–9) but they were very mild compared to the present period. This chapter attempts to investigate the effect of the crisis on the peasant economy. To what extent has this economy been affected?

The extent of the crisis

In the post-World War II period until the mid-1970s Peru experienced sustained economic growth together with price stability. The real income per capita in 1974 was twice as high as in the 1950s. Annual rates of inflation never exceeded 18%. Starting around 1974–5 the economic situation changed dramatically: the economy stagnated until 1976, and there was an absolute decline in average real income. Real GNP per capita dropped by 8% in four years and the level of real income in 1980 was barely above that already reached back in 1971. The average annual rates of inflation went from 24% in 1975 to 68% in 1979. (See Table 8.1.) Politically, a new military government came to power in mid-1975, headed by General Francisco Morales Bermudez.

The origin of the crisis is commonly associated with excess demand in the economy, especially as a result of the government's overspending. Table 8.1 shows that government deficit was around 3.1–3.9% of GNP before 1975 and jumped to 5.5–7.5% in the period 1975–8. In association with this overspending and unfavor-

Table 8.1 *Peru: indicators of economic crisis, 1970–81*

Year	Real GNP per capita (1970 = 100)	Av. annual rate of inflation (%)	Exchange rate US $ (1970 = 100)	Government deficit/GNP (%)	Trade bal./exp. (%)
1970	100	5.0	100	n.a.	32.3
1971	104	6.8	100	3.1	17.7
1972	107	7.2	100	3.7	14.1
1973	110	9.5	100	3.9	7.1
1974	114	16.9	100	3.1	− 26.8
1975	114	23.6	104	5.5	− 85.2
1976	114	33.5	160	6.3	− 54.5
1977	110	38.0	303	7.5	− 25.4
1978	104	57.8	453	5.1	17.5
1979	105	67.7	578	1.4	39.8
1980	106	59.7	791	3.4	19.7
1981	107	73.5	1,148	7.8	− 19.6

Source: Banco Central de Reserva, *Memoria* (1974–9), and Instituto Nacional de Estadística, various publications. For 1981, Banco Central, *Reseña Económica*, March 1982.

able conditions in international markets, Peru also faced an external crisis: the balance of trade was secularly negative from 1974 until 1977.[1]

Economic policies to stabilize the economy were initiated in 1973, with a selective policy of subsidies on certain products considered basic (such as foodstuffs) and price–wage controls. These policies continued throughout the period of crisis. The objective was always to reduce aggregate demand, including demand for imports. Government deficits were reduced significantly only by 1979–80 and the balance of trade turned positive only in 1978. The rate of exchange has been depreciated significantly since 1976. The period 1975–80 was dominated by economic policies leading to economic stabilization.

The average income of workers in the modern sector declined substantially. The average wage income of a typical blue-collar worker in 1980 allows him to buy only 60% of his purchasing power of 1974, as shown in Table 8.2. The fall in white-collar incomes is even more dramatic. Workers at the lower wage levels suffered relatively less. Table 8.2 shows the case of a hypothetical worker who entered a firm earning minimum wages and received wage-increases

Table 8.2 *Peru: indicators of income distribution in the modern sector 1970–80 (1970 = 100)*

Year	Average real wage income			Profits	
	White-collar	Blue-collar	Compensated low-paid[a]	Real values	Share in nat. income (%)
1970	100	100	—	100	20
1971	107	109	—	95	18
1972	115	118	—	95	18
1973	117	130	—	137	22
1974	112	128	109	157	24
1975	108	115	106	151	23
1976	93	118	102	163	24
1977	81	100	111	165	25
1978	70	90	100	180	28
1979	64	90	106	233	33
1980	68	95	111	234	32

[a] Includes 'exceptional compensations due to cost of living increases' decreed by the government and applied to a hypothetical worker who entered a private firm in January 1974 earning minimum wages.
Source: Ministerio de Trabajo for data on wages; Banco Central de Reserva for data on profits (*Memorias*) and *Analisis Laboral* for 'compensated low-paid'.

decreed by government 'to compensate for cost of living increases'. This worker has almost recovered his purchasing power in the last years. The policy to decree wage-increases in *absolute* amounts has had the effect of changing the wage structure and has protected relatively more the real income of the low-paid worker in the modern sector.

On the other hand, profits have increased continuously in real terms and in their share of national income during the crisis. The gain in real terms is shown in Table 8.2. One also notes that the share of profits in national income went from 23% in 1975 to 33% in 1979. In the middle of the crisis close to one-third of national income went to profits.[2]

Changes in incomes of urban workers outside the modern sector are much more difficult to estimate. This is a very heterogeneous social group with a variety of sources of income. The wage income of this group must have decreased. There are two reasons for this. First, the minimum wage rate has fallen in real terms (shown in Table 8.3) and this is the relevant wage rate for this social group, which mostly

Table 8.3 *Lima: minimum wage, unemployment and underemployment rates (%)*

Year	Real minimum wage rate[a]	Rate of unemployment	Rate of underemployment[b]
1974	100	n.a.	n.a.
1975	95	7.5	13.4
1976	91	6.9	15.5
1977	29	8.4	16.1
1978	64	8.0	30.0
1979	83	6.5	29.6
1980	88	7.1	24.2

[a] Base: 1974 = 100.
[b] Refers to people with incomes below minimum wages.
Source: Ministerio de Trabajo, *Situación Ocupacional*, Cuarto Trimestre 1980 (Lima: February 1981).

gets temporary jobs. Secondly, expansion of employment has been very small during this period of crisis. All this is consistent with the estimates on 'underemployment' in Lima. Table 8.3 shows that the proportion of Lima's labor force with incomes below the minimum wage increased from 13% in 1975 to 30% in 1978–9. The rate of open unemployment has not changed significantly during this period, however.

The other component, income from self-employment (particularly that associated with trading and commerce), must have permitted some degree of adjustment to prevent a further fall in total income of this social group. Hence, we may conclude that the fall in real income of the urban poor has been significant, but it was proportionately lower than that of the workers of the modern sector.

Changes in incomes of peasant families

Peasant families living in the highlands of Peru represent close to one-third of the country's population. This is the social group which lies at the bottom of the income pyramid in Peru. It is usually argued that peasants are outside the market system and that the economic crisis has no effect on them. However, no evidence has ever been presented in support of the 'outside-the-market' hypothesis. This study has shown estimates of the degree of integration to the market of peasant families in the southern sierra region of Peru. The result is that, on average, the peasant communities exchange 50% of their income and therefore dedicate the other 50% to self-consumption. With this result, which applies to the most 'traditional' peasant families in the most 'backward' region, the hypothesis of self-subsistence, outside the market, must be rejected. Peasant families are well integrated into the market system.

Two types of activities have been considered in the peasant economy: agriculture (including livestock) and all non-agriculture (manufacturing, construction, trading). A peasant family allocates its labor to produce those commodities with the help of resources that the family possesses. As a consequence of this self-employment the peasant family produces quantities of $\bar{X}_1$ and $\bar{X}_2$ during a year, in each activity. Another use of the family's labor force is to enter into labor markets and derive wages from temporary employment. There are two types of labor markets: local (within the community) and external (outside the community). Total wages earned in local markets will be equal to the wage rate (w_1) and total number of days worked (L_1). The same concepts will apply to external markets: w_2 for wage rates and L_2 for number of days employed.

Therefore, *total peasant income* will be equal to the monetary value of agricultural and non-agricultural production (valued at market prices) and the monetary income from wages. Since part of the goods produced is consumed by the family (X_1, X_2), and part is sold in the market (E_1, E_2), the total peasant income can be written as:

$$p_1 \bar{X}_1 + p_2 \bar{X}_2 + w_1 L_1 + w_2 L_2 = (p_1 X_1 + p_2 X_2)$$
$$+ (p_1 E_1 + p_2 E_2 + w_1 L_1 + w_2 L_2)$$

In this equation, self-consumption income is equal to the value of the first parenthesis. As shown in Chapter 4 this is around 50% of the total income for the typical peasant family in the southern sierra region in Peru. *Monetary peasant income* is allocated partly to buy modern inputs, X_3 (fertilizers, pesticides), and partly to buy consumption goods, X_4, and capital goods, X_5. Hence:

$$p_1 E_1 + p_2 E_2 + w_1 L_1 + w_2 L_2 = p_3 X_3 + p_4 X_4 + p_5 X_5$$
$$(0.37 + 0.24 + 0.22 + 0.17 = 0.05 + 0.90 + 0.05)$$

The numbers shown below the equation are the shares of each component in the income and expenditure side, as estimated in this study. With the help of the previous equations we can make some assessments on the possible effects of the present economic crisis on the income of peasants.

The decline in GNP has not been a result of a uniform decline in production in all sectors. Some sectors of the economy have fallen more drastically than others. The determination of these sectors will indicate where the employment effect was more severe. These sectors were construction, manufacturing and agriculture, in that order. In the cases of construction and agriculture, it is clear that the effect was negative on peasants' income: wage is earned mostly in these sectors, as shown in Chapter 5.

Changes in relative prices and wages included in the budget equation of peasant families will affect their real income in a period of inflation. To evaluate the effect of inflation on the peasants' income will require an estimate of the relative change of the five prices and two wage rates included in the budget equation. We do not have statistical evidence on these changes. However, based on some scattered pieces of information, an estimate of the possible effects will be given here.

Prices received at farm gates for agricultural goods (p_1) are not registered in any price index. The price index for food in Lima cannot be taken as a measure for this, for two reasons: first, the variations over time in the ratio of consumer's and producer's price; and secondly, the fact that a significant proportion of food consumed in Lima is not supplied by highland peasants but is imported – a large proportion of food consumed in Peru is imported. Domestic prices of food have been controlled throughout the period of crisis. On the other hand, subsidies to imported food maintained the prices of the import competing products depressed. The over-valuation of the exchange rate had the same effect. As Table 8.1 shows, the rate of inflation has been higher than the rate of devaluation, compared to 1970 parity and even to 1974 parity. In any event we can assume that p_1 increased at the same rate as the average rate of inflation, due to the relaxation in price controls, subsidies and import policies that took place in 1978–9.

With respect to p_2, the basic effect is related to the trading activity. The most important single non-agricultural source of money income is trading. The cost of trading, the price of commodities imported into the peasant communities and the cost of transportation all increased with inflation and have, possibly, created a reduction in the net income from trading.

The wage rates which are more relevant for peasants entering labor markets are the legal minimum wage. This is true for local as well as for external markets. Wage policies implemented in Peru revised periodically the level of minimum wages by regions. The result was a fourfold increase in money terms during 1975–9. Inflation in the same period implied, however, a sixfold increase in price levels. In addition, the cost of entering into external labor markets increased substantially (cost of transportation and food). All this clearly led to a relative reduction in the net money income from wages. In sum, on the income side of the budget equation, prices and wage rates increased by less than the general inflation rate (measured by the consumer's price index of Lima).

We should now review the expenditure side. Here, the relevant price is p_4, as 90% of the expenditure is allocated to the imports of consumer goods. The basic products in the imported consumption basket of the peasant family are: salt, sugar, cooking oil, rice, noodles, flour, coca, alcohol, kerosene, soaps/detergents, clothing. A price index of these commodities was constructed for the period 1973–9. It shows an index of 950 in 1979 compared to 100 in 1973 (Ruiz, 1980). This increase is much higher than the rise of the consumer's price index in Lima. The divergence occurred mainly in 1978–9 when price controls and subsidies were reduced substantially. The point is that some commodities under control were part of the basket of consumption of both urban and peasant families. When prices were freed the relative increase was higher for peasant families, compared to Lima's families, indicating that those commodities had a higher weight in their consumption basket of goods bought in the market.

The evidence on permanent migration indicates that on average every peasant family has one member (son or daughter) who lives in a city. This sole fact suggests that private transfers of income must be an important source of income for peasant families. It was shown in Chapter 5 that this income is equivalent to almost 10% of their total money income. To the question of whether transfers from their sons or daughters were increasing in the last years, the answers we got from the peasant families in the study are as follows: 11% said yes; 47% said that no significant change has occurred; and 42% said that it has decreased. They were told that the cost of living in Lima was increasing substantially and for this reason their relatives were not able to send the same income as before.

The evidence we have presented indicates that the prices of

commodities and labor sold by peasants increased by a smaller proportion than the inflation rate; on the other hand, the price of consumption goods that peasant families buy from the market increased more rapidly than the inflation rate. The fact that p_4 grew faster than the inflation rate indicates that real income, measured in terms of purchasing power of imported consumption goods (X_4) of peasant families, clearly decreased during the period of economic crisis.

We have shown that relative prices moved against peasants during the inflation period. We now need to estimate the absolute amount by which real income fell. To experience a decline of 40% in real income, as in the case of workers of the modern sector, the monetary income of peasants should have declined by 80% in real terms, since half of total income is in monetary income. For this to happen relative prices must have fallen by 80%, on average, during this period. This could not have happened. An estimate of the relative change in w_1/p_4 from 1974 to 1979 shows that this ratio fell by 33%. Taking this ratio as the average proportion in the decline of relative prices, which is still an overestimation since some prices (such as p_1) increased more rapidly than wages, would lead to an estimate of 16% in the reduction of real income during 1970–5. Including the reduction in transfers, this percentage might fall to 13–15%. This is a much smaller loss in real income compared to workers of the modern sector and to the urban poor.

The general conclusion that one may draw from these pieces of evidence is that inequality and absolute poverty in Peru increased during the crisis. The major change in inequality is between profits and incomes from labor. On the other hand, the poverty line for 1980 shows that more people are under it compared to 1974; moreover, the new families incorporated to this condition are basically urban. In sum, the shape of the income pyramid has changed in two ways: a stretch at the top and a squeeze at the bottom.

Economic policies in the early 1980s

The economic policy of the second Belaunde administration (inaugurated in July 1980) contains new elements to overcome the crisis: to liberalize the economy from price controls, tariffs and subsidies. The idea is to attain a higher level of economic efficiency in the economy. Another policy objective is to reduce inflation, mainly through cuts in government spending. The effect of gains in economic efficiency on income distribution is not easy to determine. However, Arthur Okun (1975) advances the proposition that a trade-off exists between efficiency and equality. The more equality is pursued in a market economy the less efficient becomes the economic system. Hence, the implicit choice of the present policy markets is biased against equality.

The most important policy of income redistribution now refers to food stamps. This program attempts to take income from the government budget and transfer it to the poorest families ('the extreme poverty') through food stamps. This policy will substitute the subsidies on food which were eliminated. The success of this program will depend on several things. First, this program must be massive to be effective. The experience with food stamps in countries like the United States cannot be taken as a model. In that country food stamps are aimed at a very small proportion of the population, because the poor constitute a pocket in a sea of richness. In Peru, however, we have the opposite situation: a pocket of richness in a sea of poverty. Therefore, any program designed to help the poor must be a massive one. Secondly, as indicated before, with the economic crisis changes in the income pyramid occurred. Absolute poverty increased. Approximately 50% of the population in Peru live under conditions of extreme poverty now. Hence, the redistribution program must be enormous. Thirdly, the amount of income to be transferred must be substantial. The food stamp program, however, amounts to only 2% of the total government budget for 1981. If we discount the losses that part of these funds will suffer, due to bureaucratic mismanagement and possible corruption (that is, through Okun's 'leaky bucket'), the net transfer will be very small. In fact, the value of the coupons has been set at 3,000 *soles* per month, which is equivalent to 10% of minimum wage in Lima.[3]

In terms of massive transfers, the policy of subsidies on food had a better performance. Table 8.4 shows the incidence of the food subsidies in 1980. This incidence is clearly regressive if the rural poor are excluded. However, the view taken by the government is that the program is progressive *as a whole*. The statistical base of these estimates is very weak, as it relies on a 1972 survey on food consumption. Particularly, the rural case seems underestimated. Chapter 5 showed that, on average, 50% of monetary income of the rural poor is spent on food, which implies 25% of total income, and

Table 8.4 *Food subsidy incidence by families, 1980 (soles per month)*

Strata	Population (%)	Average income	Average subsidy	Incidence (%)
High	7.0	180,000	4,200	2.3
Medium	26.5	66,500	3,000	4.5
Urban – low	20.2	38,000	4,100	10.8
Rural – low	46.3	16,000	800	5.0
	100.0			

Source: Banco Central de Reserva. Data released in a symposium on 'Nutrition and Food Subsidies', January 1981 (Webb, 1981).

most of those foodstuffs were subsidized, such as sugar, cooking oil, rice, noodles and wheat-flour.

But even if those statistical estimates are taken as good approximations, Table 8.4 shows that poor families, particularly those living in urban areas, got a higher transfer (4,100 *soles*) than the present food stamp program, which will transfer 3,000 *soles* to fewer families. The target is that at the beginning of the food stamp program 10% of total families of Peru will be reached. Hence, by substituting the food subsidy program for food stamps, the cost of redistribution is reduced from 10% of the government budget to 2%. Finally, even if the upper 50% of the income pyramid benefits more from the food subsidy program than the bottom 50%, which is actually the official argument to arrive at the conclusion that the system as a whole is progressive, it does not follow that the subsidy program should be eliminated. This progressiveness can be corrected with other policies, such as a more progressive taxation, so as to get a net transfer to the poor through the government budget.

The other argument against food subsidies is the negative effect on agricultural income. The subsidy is given to imported food, most of which competes with domestic production; thus subsidies introduce a price discrimination against domestic farmers. However, the only alternative to solve this problem is not to eliminate the subsidies. One possibility was to extend the subsidy also to the production of domestic farmers. In this manner the price discrimination that they have suffered for years could have been eliminated, and incentives to increase agricultural production could have been created. On the other hand, it was shown in Chapter 7 that the effect of increasing food prices at the farm gate on urban real income is relatively small: doubling prices would reduce that income by only 15%.

Structural stagnation in peasants' incomes

From the post-World War II period until the mid-1970s Peru experienced a variety of political regimes (liberal, interventionist, reformist); and different strategies of economic growth (export-led and import substitution). During this period substantial economic growth was achieved. Hence, Peru's economic performance has relevance for the problem of growth and equity, under different schemes, in less developed countries.

In terms of inequality Peru's performance is disappointing. The overall income inequality increased over time. Even more unfortunate is the fact that the poorest social group, the peasantry, did not benefit from the process of growth. Peasant incomes were almost stagnant during that period. Not only did distributive policies fail to reach them, but even the programs of social reforms left them almost untouched. Neither liberal nor reformist governments paid attention to this social group. Economic growth under different strategies did not have any significant effect on raising their standards of living. Capitalist development and the market mechanism also failed.

In the last five years Peru experienced another phenomenon which is also very typical of less developed countries: recession together with inflation. Real income of peasant families has decreased during the economic crisis. A 'best guess' of this decline would be 13–15% for the period 1975–80. This is a much smaller loss in real income compared to workers of the modern sector (firms with more than 10 workers), where that percentage ranged between 38% and 45%. Given this decline and the increase in real profits; and given the structure of income in that sector, the total decline in the modern sector could be estimated around 4–5%. Since almost two-thirds of national income are generated in the modern sector, the rest (the 'traditional sector') must have decreased by 17%. Only then would the weighted average of both sectors give 8% as a result. Thus, it seems that peasant families, medium-sized farmers and urban workers outside the modern sector all experienced a decrease in income of the order of 17%.

The lowest percentage in the reduction of real income in the traditional sector seems therefore to apply to peasant families. The fact that, recently, many people have returned to the peasant communities because of the economic difficulties they faced in the cities is consistent with this conclusion. Or it may be that these returns show that the conditions of urban workers in the traditional sector are much more precarious in the city than in the countryside. So, even a similar percentage decrease in real income causes a more serious problem to the urban poor than to the rural poor. The rural poor have, on one hand, a more diversified economy which reduces the risk of any major change in their economic situation; on the other hand, the family can return to the 'natural economy' if it becomes difficult to buy commodities. There is certainly a much lower floor of subsistence income in the countryside.[4]

The economic policies initiated in the second half of 1980 give higher priority to efficiency, as opposed to equality, and to the controlling of inflation, particularly in regard to the reduction of the government deficit. However, in view of the increase in absolute poverty during this economic crisis, redistributive policies have a substantial role to play in the present economic policy of Peru. This does not imply a disequilibrium in the government budget. It does imply a fiscal policy oriented toward redistribution, through a change in the structure of spending accordingly, and/or through a tax reform to finance redistributive programs. The conspicuous consumption of the rich in Peru, even in the middle of the economic crisis, is a clear indication that there is enough room for significant income redistribution.

9

Conclusions: reality, theory and policy

This study has been concerned with the functioning of the peasant economy in today's Peru. This particular reality has been neglected in the economic studies on Peru, in spite of its great significance in the social system. The peasant economy has remained a reality without a theory. In this study the basic traits of the peasant economy have been investigated and then utilized to lay down the principal analytical coordinates of its prevailing economic rationality. The peasant economy has also been placed in the context of capitalist development in order to analyze its changing role in the economic system. In this final chapter a summary of our empirical findings and theoretical interpretations are presented. This will be done in terms of the hypotheses advanced in Chapter 2. Because a theoretical basis has been reached, economic policies are also discussed.

Poor but efficient

The economy of the peasant communities in the Peruvian sierra is organized in family units, which are the units of production and consumption. In the case of the southern sierra, the most economically depressed area, the average size of the peasant family varies between four and five members; the average total labor force is four people and the adult labor force is two. The peasant family depends upon resources of cultivable land, and usually has no more than five hectares in area in addition to access to natural pastures, communally held. The cultivable land is composed of parcels, the average number of which varies between ten and 80, depending upon the community. Regarding livestock, a peasant family typically has seven sheep, two heads of cattle and one horse. Finally, they generally own three shovels, picks, and other minor tools.

The empirical data cited demonstrates the tiny size of the peasant

114

production unit. The peasant family of the Peruvian sierra is a *minifundista* family. Its resources are assigned to the production of agricultural (A) and livestock (P) goods, to a series of non-agricultural activities which we have called Z-activities. Family labor is allocated partly to self-employment in the economic unit and partly to wage labor through temporary employment in labor markets (L). Besides being small, the peasant economic unit is very diversified in its productive activities.

Not only is the quantity of resources at the command of a peasant family small, their quality is very low. The level of their education is certainly low: approximately 75% of the heads of peasant families surveyed have not finished primary school. The cultivable lands are of low quality; the greater part is without water and located on steep slopes. The communal pastures are also of the poorest quality. Seen in the perspective of the sierra economy as a whole, and that of Peru, the peasant economy truly operates on marginal lands. The quality of the livestock is also low if compared to other productive units in Peru. Moreover, the equipment used to produce Z-goods still relies on traditional technology.

In addition, in the technology utilized, there is an absence of modern inputs. The use of fertilizers and pesticides is the most widespread, but the proportion of families involved is still small; furthermore, they are applied without any technical assistance. The use of new varieties of seeds, of improved species of livestock, of improved cultivated pastures is absent. On the whole, it is evident that the peasant economy depends upon poor resources and traditional technology.

There is no evidence that the peasant economy is inefficient. With the resources and technical knowledge they currently possess, it is difficult to imagine ways of significantly increasing production or their income. Regarding technical efficiency, two aspects of the peasant economy are commonly cited as examples of the possibility of increasing production, even with existing resources and technology. The first concerns the fragmentation of cultivable land. Considering the risk and uncertainty involved in sierra agriculture, however, fragmentation is a very rational response. The peasant's economic behavior – of aversion to risk – is not a personal characteristic but rather a social characteristic. It is a rational response to the social, economic and geographic conditions in which the peasantry operates. It is possible that the fragmentation might be excessive in some cases, in relation to the risk to be covered, but there is no clear evidence that by joining the parcels one would be able to increase total output significantly.

The second case of alleged inefficiency refers to the wastefulness of some agricultural activities, which take the form of fiestas. One may observe that the corn harvest, for example, is brought in by more hands than is technologically necessary and consumes more goods than is necessary for the maintenance of the labor force, but this does not necessarily imply inefficiency. Inefficiency is a relevant concept when the process of production and consumption are socially separate. It is a characteristic of the peasant economy that these processes are integrated; consumption and production are, in many cases, intertwined activities. This is certainly a substantive difference from the capitalist economy, in which these activities are dis-associated. The 'circular flow' between families and enterprises employed by economics texts to represent the functioning of the capitalist economy is not, therefore, applicable to the peasant economy.

Concerning economic efficiency – meaning that prices and costs should be incorporated into the decision-making process of the economic unit in order to obtain the maximum net income from every allocation of resources – it is commonly thought that the peasant family follows a 'traditional' economic behavior, in the sense that it does not evaluate new market situations and does not respond to price incentives. 'They always do the same', it is said. Besides the fact that, with changes in prices, one cannot continue 'doing the same' because the given bundle of commodities is no longer attainable or there will be income in excess, which demands readjustments in the quantities produced and consumed, there is empirical evidence which shows variability in the annual crop mix, in the periods in which products might be sold, and in the migration periods among peasant families. The simple fact that the families are very different in their sources of income is an indication that there is no 'traditional' behavior in the communities. On the contrary, everything is subject to continuous economic evaluation.

On the other hand, it is also true that there is a certain inelasticity in the production of a product, should its price rise. But this inelasticity is not the result of a 'traditional' behavior; it is, rather, a rational response in a context of decisions made in the face of risk and uncertainty. Should the price of potatoes rise in one period, all the peasants are not going to plant more potatoes, neglecting a well-established balance in their portfolio of crops. They obviously can have no certainty that those new prices will prevail in the next period. With clear indications of the direction of relative prices the peasant economy responds in a 'viscous' way, as it must revise an entire portfolio, carefully established and tested. Conceptually, viscosity has been confused for traditional behavior.

Thus, to attribute the poverty of the peasant economy to inefficiency in the productive process is due to a conceptional confusion. The low physical productivity is explained principally by the quantity and quality of the resources and technology available in the peasant economy. It is clear that with different resources and different technology, production would be greater, but this effect does not correspond to the concept of efficiency. If to this fact one adds the economic behavior characterized by aversion to risk, which is a response to the geographic and social context in which the peasant economy operates, much of what seems to be economic inefficiency reduces almost to nothing. The peasant families of the sierra are, in conclusion, poor but efficient. Thus they conform to the thesis of Professor Schultz (1964).

Relative overpopulation

The hypothesis that there is a permanent excess of labor in the peasant communities does not seem to be correct either. The empirical results shown here indicate that the labor of the peasant family is dedicated to diverse activities. If the marginal productivity of labor is zero, as the surplus labour hypothesis implies, this means it is zero in *all* the activities (A, P, Z and L). It is possible that the marginal productivity of labor might be zero if the entire labor force were dedicated to a *single* activity. This is precisely the conceptual error incurred in all the studies which attempt to measure excess peasant labor with reference to the requirements of labor only in agriculture and livestock production. But if one takes into account *all* activities, the marginal productivity rises. The hypothesis of an *order* in the use of labor, first in $A - P$ and then in $Z - L$, implies that the marginal productivity could be lower in $A - P$, as this productivity's variance is less than in the case of $Z - L$, but not to the point of being zero. In addition, the fact that the wages in local and external labor markets constitute opportunity cost demonstrates that the marginal productivities in A, P and Z cannot be zero.

Another proof that no excess of labor exists, at least in significant amounts, is that the wage rates in the peasant communities tend to rise during periods of peak agricultural activity. As shown in this study, during harvest time it is common to pay wages in products, whose market value is superior to the monetary wage ruling in the other months. Moreover, the employers (proprietors of medium-sized farms) resort to a series of mechanisms in their personal relations to assure themselves of labor in 'times of scarcity'.

Finally, the evidence found that the temporary migration to labor markets external to the community is *seasonal* again points to the refutation of the overpopulation hypothesis. If it had been observed that temporary migration took place at any time of year, this would have indicated the existence of a structural surplus of labor. Nonetheless, the scarcity of labor in periods of peak agricultural activity and the temporary migration at other times offer clear indications that there is no such structural surplus. That which seems to be an excess of labor, at least to people unfamiliar with the rural economy, is the fact that the peasants are not occupied in agricultural activities during the entire year. Seasonal agricultural unemployment is thus confused for structural unemployment.

It is true, on the other hand, that areas of *minifundio* show a greater population density than areas of modern economic units. But this obeys the different rationality of the peasant economy, compared to the capitalist enterprise. The peasant economy is sustained by the control of the land, and the size of the labor force tends, therefore, to coincide with the *greatest* demand for labor in the annual agricultural cycle, assigning the seasonally unemployed labor to Z-activities and temporary migrations. In a capitalist context, the same quality of land and the same cyclical requirements for labor would involve employing a permanent labor force at the *minimum* of the cyclical requirements, covering the greater seasonal requirements by contracting temporary labor. This is the way the enterprise minimizes costs.[1]

If the productivity of labor does not qualify the peasant communities as an overpopulated economy, the level of their productivity is in most cases below subsistence income. The most plausible hypothesis is that *absolute* overpopulation does not exist, but *relative* overpopulation does. The fact that wage income is an important source in the total peasant income implies that the peasant family in general cannot derive even a subsistence income by the exploitation of their *own* resources. Their plot would not give them enough to subsist upon, even if they dedicated all their time to self-employment.

Therefore, it is entry into the labor market which allows them, through a division of family labor, to ensure a subsistence income. This is the role played by labor markets in the functioning of the peasant economy. The economic viability of the peasant economy is, thus, assured by this mechanism.

Non-capitalist relations

The idea that most peasant families are integrated into the hacienda system by means of pre-capitalist relations has been very widespread in Peru. This concept has given rise to the idea that the poverty of the peasantry is a consequence of the servile mechanisms of the haciendas. It is indubitably true that these servile forms still exist but their significance is minor for a comprehension of the peasant economy in its totality.

One evidence of the reduced link between the peasant economy and the sierra hacienda in the productive process is seen in the extent of the agrarian reform program. This program affected almost all the medium-sized and large haciendas of the sierra, the beneficiaries being close to 120,000 families which live in peasant communities. But this figure greatly exaggerates the number of beneficiaries as it includes the SAIS system, a type of cooperative, in which various communities surrounding the hacienda were incorporated as members of the new enterprise. A more appropriate figure for measuring the nexus between peasant families and haciendas in non-capitalist relations would be approximately 80,000, which is roughly 10% of the population of peasant families in the sierra. The essential aspect of today's peasant economy is its relations of exchange through the market. This is true even for the period before the agrarian reform.

Integration into the market system

Another widespread opinion on the peasant economy is that it is isolated from the rest of the national economy. 'Self-sufficient economies' and 'economies outside the market' are two of the phrases that sum up this thesis. This also gives rise to the idea that Peru is a 'dual economy', that is to say, separated, its parts unconnected. One of those parts is certainly the peasant economy of the sierra. This is the common view of the Peruvian economy and society, as of the other Andean countries. The statistical results of the present study, however, give a very different picture.

The peasant family produces A, P and Z-goods with its own resources and labor. Another source of income is that obtained through employment as wage-earners in the local and external labor markets. Part of its production of A, P and Z is sold in the market and part is consumed by the family itself. The monetary value of everything produced as goods A, P and Z plus the monetary income from wage employment constitutes the *total peasant income*. If one divides this income between the part that the family consumes and the part that it exchanges with the market (as much of goods A, P and Z as of labor) the resulting proportion for a typical family of the southern sierra is 50:50. In as much as half of the peasant income in the most traditional region of Peru is the result of exchange with the market, there is no basis to the thesis of 'self-sufficiency' or 'duality'. One speaks of countries as 'open economies' when they export 15–20% of their Gross National Product. Nonetheless, the peasant economy has been seen as 'closed economy' despite the fact that it exports around 50% of its total product. It seems that cultural and social duality, which clearly exists in Peru, has been confused with economic duality.

The structure of the *monetary income* of the typical peasant family of the southern sierra is 37% from sales of A and P, 24% from Z (where an important proportion is income from commercial activities), 22% from wage employment in local markets and 17% from external markets, reached by seasonal migrations. Thus approximately 40% of the peasants' monetary income is from wage employment. The peasant family today is also proletarian. These sources of income demonstrate, then, the principal characteristics of the peasant economy in its present historical form in Peru.

The real income of the peasant family therefore depends in part on the price system of the market. Changes in the prices of agricultural goods that they produce, or in the prices of the products that they buy, and changes in the wage rates in rural and urban labor markets, cause significant changes in the peasant income. As market prices are modified as a consequence of, among other things, changes in macro-economic policies, price controls and international prices, it is clear that the peasant economy is integrated into the national and international economy. The integration or articulation is achieved through the products markets and the labor markets. The poverty of the peasants must then be explained within the income distribution mechanism that operates in the Peruvian economy.

Dynamics of the peasant economy

In the peasant economy land and other resources have remained almost fixed while population has increased. This implies a diminution in the *minifundio* size per family. If one also considers the fact that the resources have been deteriorating in quality (as seen in the erosion of land, the overgrazing of pasture lands, the invasion of weeds in a large part of those lands), the aforementioned conclusion is reinforced. The recent introduction of certain modern inputs, such as fertilizers and pesticides, has at the most somewhat counteracted these effects. Productivity increases have clearly been practically nil.

The conclusion from above is, hence, inescapable: over time each peasant family produces less output than before in its own unit of production. It also follows that over time, given the relative market prices, the capacity of the *minifundio* to reproduce the peasant family is more limited. The peasant family has therefore only two alternatives: to emigrate, or – if staying in the rural area – to find additional income as wage labor in temporary jobs. In this way, by a growing process of proletarianization the peasants' supply of labor to temporary labor markets is increased.

The growing process of proletarianization of the peasantry is not the consequence of its population growth only. The pattern of capitalist development also plays a significant role here. Two arguments can be presented to support this view. First, the degree of the peasant economy's integration into the market economy has increased over time. The proportion of monetary income in the peasants' total income has risen in the past decades; the peasant economy interacts with the market much more now than in the 1940s, for example.

To the degree that market exchange expands in the national economy, the structure of the peasant economy will tend to be modified as well. A higher level of exchange was not the consequence of higher levels of productive capacity in the peasant economy. It was the result of increased opportunities to exchange through markets, mainly due to improvements in transportation and communication systems. It was the result of a 'commercial revolution' and not of an 'economic revolution'. Hence more market exchange for the peasant family implied either a reduction in the level of own-consumption or a reallocation of labor. It seems that the second effect has been dominant. In fact, several anthropological and sociological studies have shown a significant change in the rural life in the sierra since the 1940s, particularly in terms of growing penetration of manufactured goods (Quijano, 1968). Thus a clear consequence of the expansion of capitalism is the destruction of rural industry, the Z-activities.[2] Therefore, to pay for the increasing imports peasants have reallocated their family labor from Z-goods to wage employment.

Secondly, peasant agricultural and livestock production (potatoes, corn, barley, wheat, milk, meat, wool) competes in the urban markets with capitalist production. As shown in this study, the development of productive forces is very rapid in the agriculture of developed countries and food is increasingly imported into Peru. Also capitalist domestic agriculture has shown some improvements in productivity. But the peasant economy is almost stagnant. As a consequence there has been a decline in the proportion of agricultural output produced in the peasant economy, from 49% in 1948–52 to 31% in 1967–71 (Hopkins, 1981: p. 69). The peasant economy has lost significance as a food supplier to urban markets. Capital accumulation and technological change in Peru have been concentrated in the capitalist sector, leaving aside the peasant economy.

The proletarianization process of the peasantry also indicates a change in its role in the economic system. Previously, its role was to contribute to the supply of cheap foodstuffs for the cities, so as to keep urban wages down. Now, it is becoming more a source of cheap labor directly. If it were not for the *minifundio*, labor could not be hired at minimum daily wage for only a certain period and then laid off. Because the worker has an economic unit to return to once his labor contract is terminated, the labor market for casual employment can exist. Moreover, this is a very cheap system for the capitalist firms because they pay as wages only part of the annual cost needed to reproduce that labor force. The other part comes from self-employment in the *minifundio*. Hence the peasantry helps to keep wages down directly. In this sense, the peasant economy performs the role of the 'reserve army' in the present historical stage of Peru's capitalist development.

In sum, the processes of population growth and capitalist development generate an increasing degree of proletarianization of the peasantry, an increasing need of wage income and wage employment. But, where will the demand for labor come from? The capitalist development has a limited capacity to generate the needed wage income. First, wage employment in Peru has remained stagnant in relative terms; the 'modern sector' employed 21% of the labor force in 1961 and 1970 (Webb, 1977: Table 6.1). Secondly, peasants compete for wage income in rural and urban labor markets and these markets are becoming saturated due to population growth and migration. Thirdly, the historical experience shown in this study indicates that although the capitalist sector grew at rapid rates the peasant economy stagnated. The *capitalist road* to development has not induced overall growth, as many people expected; in particular it has not induced growth for the rural poor.

Some implications for economic policies

Given the limited capacity of the capitalist development to induce economic growth for the peasantry, why not develop the peasant economy *directly*? By increasing productivity and income from self-employment in the *minifundio* less will be needed of wage employment. Economic policy could be directed toward reversing the current economic process: make the peasant family more farmer and less proletarian. This *peasant road* to overcome rural poverty will also have a positive effect on wage rates: labor supply will decrease and real wages can rise in urban and rural labor markets.

The results of the present study have many implications for the design of economic policies for improving the economic condition of the peasant economy. In what follows, brief mention will be made of the most notable implications. First, and the most obvious, is to increase the amount of land to peasant families. However, this would require an extremely careful policy designed to get land from units with 'excess' land and to transfer that land to families with the greatest need. The issue is difficult because this policy implies a step beyond the agrarian reform recently completed, but the effects can be significant for the peasantry (Figueroa, 1982).

Secondly, the sources of the total peasant income are very diverse. Economic policies (designed to improve their income) which are based on one product, such as a corn program, or based on one activity, such as a program fostering artisanry, would have only a small effect in proportion to its importance in the structure of income. Economic policies must cover a broader range than one price or product if they are to have real effect upon the peasants' income.

From this perspective, there are two policies which would have a significant effect. The first concerns the pricing of agricultural and livestock goods. If one were to raise these prices, relative to the *entirety of goods*, there would be two effects on the peasants' income: one, direct, through their sale of those goods, and the other indirect, by means of their wage income. The wage income obtained by the peasants comes principally from two activities: agriculture and construction, as much in local as external labor markets. Greater profitability would then foster agricultural growth and greater employment which would increase the salary income of the peasant family. And the supply of rural labor lies in the *minifundios*.

The other policy concerns credit. The peasant families need credit for their diverse activities: purchase of agricultural inputs, of tools, of livestock, and of raw materials for artisanry, working-capital for commerce and working-capital for migration to external labor markets. The specific necessities of each family are different, and therefore credit supplied to one sector alone, for example, agricultural credit, would not give the peasant family flexibility in its use. One would have to think in terms of a policy of *peasant credit* in response to the needs of the *peasant economy*.

Thirdly, as the technology is still traditional there is room for improvement of the physical productivity in peasant communities. This implies modernization through the introduction of new and modern inputs in the production of A, P and Z-goods. Modernization, however, does not simply, or necessarily, mean the introduction of fertilizers and pesticides. Modernization has more meaning when there is a blend of modern inputs and *improved* traditional inputs. Improved seeds, improved livestock and improved pastures are some examples of what could be introduced in the peasant communities. The technological change with the greatest impact (and greatest diffusion) in the Andes would have to be directed principally toward the genetic improvement of Andean crops and products, that is to say those products which are already adapted to the peasant economy, ecologically and socially, through a historical process.

Technical assistance is also lacking in the peasant communities. Every community studied has its irrigation or mineral exploitation project which needs only technical direction to bring it to fruition. Disease control for plants and animals is practically non-existent because there are no technical assistance or extension programs. On the other hand, neither technical development nor programs of technical diffusion are designed in terms of the peasant economy. For example, research on new varieties concentrate mainly in increasing its *average* yield, but not to reduce its *variance* (risk).

Modernization is an obvious way to raise the peasants' income. The results of the present study in this sense corroborate Professor Schultz's thesis. But they also point out two important differences : on the one hand, modernization implies also a qualitative improvement in traditional inputs or in their supply (the supply of water, for example); on the other hand, given that the peasants' income depends as much on the productivity of self-employed labor as on the price system, modernization cannot be judged solely as a technical problem. Gains in productivity could simply be transferred to the cities by the price mechanism if they are, at the same time, accompanied by a policy of anti-rural prices.

Appendix I: The sample

The empirical study of peasant communities was undertaken in the southern sierra region of Peru. Eight communities were studied. These communities were picked from a sample universe which constituted the most important community areas in the southern sierra. Preliminary studies were conducted in seven of these communities before September 1978, at which time was begun the fieldwork for the present study. The communities studied are located in four of five departments comprising the southern sierra; Ayacucho is the department not represented. This does not, however, present any particular complication to the problems of sample representativity in as much as the differences between departments are of minor importance.

The empirical data were obtained via a peasant family survey, administered as a uniform questionnaire in all of the peasant communities. Interviews were also conducted with persons involved in the life of the community (mainly authorities and ex-authorities) from which were obtained a physical and social perspective which was of great importance in sharpening the contents of the interview to be administered to the families. This procedure also permitted the control of the quality of the interviews by the range of possibilities for response which was given by notable persons. In each community the survey itself (apart from previous visits) lasted approximately two weeks and was conducted, on average, by four persons, three of whom (including the principal researcher) constituted a permanent team, the fourth interviewer usually being a person from the community. The interviews took place in Quechua or Aymara when the family surveyed did not have sufficient command of Spanish.

After concluding the fieldwork in each community, reports were written describing all that was observed during the stay in the community. These reports constitute valuable material for the analysis of the quantitative data.

The total number of families surveyed was 306, distributed among eight peasant communities as detailed in Table 2.3, p. 12. Furthermore, two more qualitative studies treating specific themes were undertaken in two peasant communities: rural artisanry in San Pedro, in the department of Cuzco; and migrations in Accomayo, in the department of Ayacucho.

In each peasant community the sample was obtained after estimating the total population. The predetermined sample size was around 40 families. This size permits statistical analysis for each community and, at the same time, permits information collection in a more detailed and profound manner from each family. The sampling, including the selection of reemplacements, was random. The first three rows of

Table A.1 *Expansion of the sample (number of families)*

Communities	Ecological level I			Ecological level II				Ecological level III	Total
	JAC	CUL	NIN	ANC	TTI	SIH	HUA	ACO	
Sample size (n)	36	40	31	40	36	41	42	40	306
Population (N)	180	290	42	180	92	322	304	100	1,510
$\alpha = N/n$	5.0	7.25	1.35	4.5	2.55	7.85	7.24	2.5	4.93
Population (N)		512				898		100	1,510
Southern sierra population (M)		110,000				320,000		70,000	500,000
$\beta = M/N$		215				356		700	331
$\alpha\beta = M/n$	1,075	1,559	290	1,602	908	2,795	2,577	1,750	1,632
Southern sierra population (M)	39	62	9	64	33	115	108	70	500

Table A.1 show the sample size in community (n), the total population of families (N), and the respective coefficient of expansion (α) for the eight communities studied.

The expansion of the sample to the southern sierra region required various steps. In the first place, the total population of the region was estimated based on the population and agricultural censuses, both from 1972. There are around one million *minifundista* peasants (with fewer than five hectares of land) in Peru; 82% live in the sierra (Figueroa, 1976).

On the other hand, from the same population census it can be inferred that a little less than 50% of the rural sierra population is located in the southern sierra region. Nevertheless, without more precise information it was assumed that the proportion of sierra peasant families which is located in the southern sierra is much greater than 50%, due to the predominately *minifundista* character of the region. An estimate of 60% appears more appropriate. This implies an estimate of 500,000 peasant families living in the southern sierra of Peru.

Secondly, the expansion requires the taking into account of ecological 'levels' (*pisos*). The productive structure (and the income structure) of the peasant economy depends on the community's access to different kinds of land, on control of different ecological levels. A community which has no access to the *quechua* zone, for example, would not produce corn, as was indicated in Chapter 2. In that the intent of this study is the estimation of peasant family income structure, the communities' access to different ecological levels becomes an important variable in the expansion of the sample. The communities Jacantaya, Culta and Ninamarca are typical of the *suni* zone; Acobamba is typical of the *yunga* zone and the rest of the communities are typical of the *quechua* zone.

The communities under study control various ecological levels and, as such, the families surveyed represent distinct proportions of the population. The Peruvian rural population distribution by ecological levels is presented in Chapter 2. Based on this information, 500 families were distributed in three ecological levels: *suni*, *quechua* and *yunga*. Rows 4 and 5 of Table A.1 present the sample and population distribution and by ecological levels, while row 6 depicts the respective expansion coefficients.

Therefore, the sample expansion to the southern sierra population is obtained by multiplying α and β. The number of families (M) that each sample family represents appears in the final row of Table A.1.

Appendix II: Methodological notes concerning the calculation of peasant income

1. Agricultural production measures the quantity harvested (in dry and in grain). Moreover it refers to the 'overall' harvest and not the minor harvest, included in green. There is certainly an underestimation of production.

2. The monetary income from wages derived from migration involves expenditures. It is thus necessary to distinguish between gross and net wages. Here the data are *net*. This produces an underestimation of the degree of monetization of the peasant economy. In particular some expenditure categories were underestimated, such as travel, lodging, food and beverages. The 'number of workdays' refers to days of absence from the community. During migration, the peasant faces days without work as well as days of intense work, be it in two jobs (night-watchman and day-ditchdigger) or doing overtime. Therefore, it is not permissible to obtain wage rates dividing total net income by number of days in migration.

3. The monetary and non-monetary incomes derived via the local labor market include only wages. Goods such as food, coca, cigarettes and *aguardiente* which the wage-earner receives from his/her employer are not included.

4. A, P and Z monetary incomes refer to 'value of sales'. Neither monetary costs incurred via input expenditures (fertilizers, pesticides and others) nor marketing costs (such as transport) were deducted. In the case of transport, it was considered as a consumption expenditure (to make purchases or to go on vacation) because there always exists the possibility of selling the goods in the local market.

5. Monetary income from commerce is net. If a family markets its own product we consider as A, P or Z income, according to the case, the opportunity cost of its production and *only* the surplus as income from commerce.

6. The only income which is not net refers to A, P and Z-goods. As such, the estimate presented in the text is called 'gross' monetary income.

7. Trade via barter is evaluated at the average price in force in the local market or some relevant zonal market. Barter for urban goods (sugar, noodles, oil) is considered as a monetary transaction. These cases are rare and, on the other hand, the prices implicit in the trade do not vary much from the market price.

8. To evaluate own-consumption, we used the average prices of monetary transactions and barter.

9. The estimation of the matrix which appears in Table 4.1 is based on the survey data, with the exception of the following: eggs, milk and wool were estimated based on family animal stocks and typical yields of the community; the assignment of agricultural production to direct consumption and to feed was estimated under the

assumption of a relation of 4:1 for all the communities. The latter is based on information collected at various stages of the fieldwork.

10. The manner in which monetary expenditures and incomes are estimated produces an overestimation of expenditures in relation to income. In that the period of study was one year (over which time were distributed expenditures and income), income was measured at different times during the year, while expenditures (in their most important rubrics, such as food), were measured for the week or month preceding the survey. Based on these reference periods (week or month), we extrapolated to the *entire* year. This method has the defect of exaggerating annual expenditure when there is significant inflation. Expenditures are evaluated at the prices of the most recent week (or month) but incomes are evaluated at prices of different periods. The fact that in the majority of cases the average monetary expenditure in the communities was greater than the respective income appears to be consistent with the above-mentioned bias.

11. In the face of discrepancies between the total value of exports and imports, it was assumed that export values were more trustworthy. The level of imports (which was always greater than that of exports) was then reduced to the level of exports, without modifying its structure.

Appendix III: Andean food plants

1. Potatoes: *Solanum* spp., the majority of native potatoes grown in Peru; *Solanum tuberosum* subspecies *indigena*.
2. Oca: *Oxalis tuberosa*.
3. Olluco: *Ullucus tuberosus*.
4. Mashua: *Tropaeolum tuberosum*.
5. Achira: *Canna edulis*.
6. Quinua: *Chenopodium quinoa*.
7. Cañihua: *Chenopodium pallidicaule*.
8. Achita: achis = quihuicha. *Amaranthus caudatus*.
9. Maize: *Zea mays*.
10. Tarhui: *Lupinus mutabilis*.

Appendix IV: Methodology used in the calculation of Table 7.1

1. Growth

The series of real GNP per capita estimates for the period 1950–74 was obtained from the *Cuentas Nacionales* published by the Banco Central de Reserva del Perú in various volumes (1950–65, 1960–7, 1960–9, 1960–74). For the period 1975–80, we used the series published by the Banco Central in its annual *Memorias*.

2. Inflation

The index is the Lima CPI. Published data obtained from the Instituto Nacional de Estadística were used for the entire period. (The Institute's name changed at various points during the period.)

3. Growth pattern

The series of manufactures and exports as percentages of GNP were obtained from the same sources that were used for the GNP series. In the case of exports there was no significant discrepancy between the *Cuentas Nacionales* and the *Memorias* during the period of superposition in the calculations (1972–4). Thus both series were used as if there were only one. In the case of manufactures there were discrepancies between the sources during 1972–4. The figures which appear in the *Cuentas Nacionales* are, on average, 83% of the figures in the *Memorias*. In order to have a long-term series which did not display important methodological changes in the calculations, it was considered appropriate to correct the figures in the *Memorias* by that coefficient (83%) for 1975–80.

4. Income distribution

National income and functional distribution

The series of national income and firms' profits were obtained from the *Cuentas Nacionales* and the *Memorias* of the Banco Central. Both estimates coincide for the period 1970–4. Thus it was assumed that for the period 1975–80 we could expand the series with the data of the *Memorias*. The profits data refer to total profits, without deducting taxes nor revaluation adjustments for inventories.

The profits figure for 1980 indicates insignificant growth in real terms. If it is

132

related to the data on profit taxes ('tax on juridical persons' published by the Banco Central) we find that nearly 19% of profits went to tax payments. Nevertheless, this percentage never exceeded 11% during 1974–9. This discrepancy suggests that the profits data for 1980 were underestimated. No tax reform of significance took place which could have caused the percentage to change so drastically. Even so, the profits figure for 1980 was maintained; this gave greater solidity to the conclusion that the change in profits during the crisis was substantial.

Incomes of workers in the 'modern sector'

This series refers to incomes from wages for workers and salaries for employees in firms with more than 10 workers. Two sources were used for the period 1950–66: the study of Richard Webb (1977), which indicates an annual growth rate of 4.1% in real terms for this period; and the series published by the Ministerio de Trabajo, Dirección General de Empleo, *Encuestas de Establecimientos*, which refers to Metropolitan Lima. These latter publications present a series starting in 1957, for which it was possible to obtain estimates for real wages and salaries for 1957–66; this implied as a result a smaller growth rate, nearly 3.2%. For the period 1967–80, we used the series from the Ministerio de Trabajo.

Incomes in the 'urban traditional sector'

For the period 1950–66, we used the estimate made by Webb (1977) which showed growth in average real income totalling 2.1% per year. For 1967–70 we assumed that there occurred a similar growth in national per capita income, for lack of additional information. Starting in 1970 we used the evolution of the legal minimum wage for Metropolitan Lima as an indicator of the average income in urban employment which was not in firms employing more than 10 workers. This series was obtained from the review *Analisis Laboral*, January 1981, p. 8. To convert this series to real terms we used the Metropolitan Lima CPI.

Incomes in the 'rural traditional sector'

Webb's estimates (1977) for the period 1950–66 were also used in this income rubric; he estimated an average annual growth rate in real income of 1.3%. For the period 1971–4, we used the growth rate of 1% per year, based on the author's evaluation of the impact of agricultural price policies on rural incomes (Figueroa, 1981). Finally, the arguments presented in the text (Chapter 8) imply an estimate of −2.7% as the change per year in real income during 1975–80.

Thus, the estimates of workers' incomes are based on various assumptions and derived from several sources of varying quality and trustworthiness. However, they were performed independently for the three sectors. A consistency analysis was undertaken in order to verify whether the real income series per sector, weighted by worker population per sector and then summed, produce values approaching total labor income estimated via the functional distribution. The latter analysis, performed for various years, displays errors of varying magnitudes (between −2% and 15%); however, the estimates appear acceptable as first approximations.

Notes

3 The economic unit and economic organization

1 The *laymi* land always starts production with potatoes, followed by cereals. After 3–4 years of cultivation the land is again left fallow for 5–10 years, depending on the quality of the land and its scarcity in the community.

2 There are communal cultivable lands in some communities which are distributed annually among peasant families, but these communities are very few.

4 Production and exchange

1 An exception is Jacantaya, where inputs are imported for boat construction and repairs. This community, located on the shore of Lake Titicaca, uses boats for transportation and for fishing.

5 The level and structure of peasant income

1 Because imported inputs are allocated basically to agriculture, the total value of these imports was deducted from the gross sales of agricultural products in order to arrive at net peasant income.

2 Data on rents are very weak. There are too many ways of paying rents and too many things rented to get good estimates. However, incomes from rent are not an important source due, in part, to the fact that most rent is paid with other productive services.

3 The difference between the income structure of the community and that of the family is due, technically speaking, to the fact that 'the ratio of means' is not the same as 'means of ratios'. If, for example, wage income is more important for poor families than for rich ones, this type of income will have a lower share in the income structure of the community compared to the family. The first case is weighted by income, the second by number of families. A comparison of the two measures therefore indicates how the different types of income are distributed among income strata. A family budget study in Lima showed little difference between the two structures – 54% and 57% for the case of wage income, for example (Figueroa, 1974). Thus, the assumption of considering both structures very similar in the case of peasant incomes, where levels and sources of income are less heterogeneous than in the case of Lima, seems reasonable.

134

6 The economic behavior of the peasant family

1 The mix of A, P, L and Z-activities and the variety of products implied in each activity show a highly diversified portfolio. Yet diversification is more than that. Even in one single product diversification is present. For example, potatoes are cultivated using a mix of varieties with different yields and resistance power to frost.

2 This behavior is consistent with the use of credit. Peasants who obtain credit from the agrarian development bank for the purchase of agricultural inputs usually allocate part of the credit to other activities, although it is illegal to do so.

3 No estimates were made about the number of days worked in the local labor market. A best guess would be to assume at *least* an equal number of temporary migration for all communities. Hence, above 25% of the labor time of the household head is probably allocated to work outside the parcel.

4 On the evolution of the labor markets in rural Peru see Cotlear (1979).

5 Another consequence of the empirical result of Table 6.4 is that the rural–urban link takes on a new form: income from transfers. We showed in the previous chapter the importance which transfers have for the income of peasant families.

6 On the peasant family strategy regarding emigration and returns see Vega (1979).

7 Stagnation in the peasant economy and the role of demand

1 Several studies support these conclusions. See, for example, Hunt (1975), Roemer (1970), Thorp and Bertram (1978).

2 If ownership of an automobile is taken as the criterion for belonging to the 'middle class', the result is exactly 5% of all families, as much in 1961 as in 1980.

3 This result was obtained from the fact that the share of profits in national income rose slightly during the period (see Table 7.1) and from the assumption, which appears reasonable, that the population of 'capitalist families' grew less than the total Peruvian population.

4 For an empirical support of this statement see Weisskoff and Figueroa (1977).

5 Estimates of income elasticities for food and other consumer goods for 10 Latin American cities can be seen in Musgrove (1978).

6 Given the tremendous dispersion of producing units and the significant real costs involved in moving commodities due to poor conditions in the systems of transport and also given imperfect market structures, these coefficients are underestimates of true values. However, this will give a bias in favor of a smaller difference between curves R and E in Figure 7.1, which we are trying to challenge.

7 An implication of this result is that the city–countryside conflict is not as acute as it is usually said to be. The prices for the food sold by rural people could be doubled and their income doubled, yet urban real income would decline by only 15%. There is much room for income redistribution through price policies for food. A further development of these issues can be seen in Figueroa (1981).

8 The substitution of agricultural food by processed food seems also related to another much deeper trend in the Latin American economies: the *irrevocable* expansion of the market system. This expansion requires an increasing amount of

processed goods. A more recent, and related, phenomenon is the presence of multinational corporations in the food processing industry.

9 A study made by Alvarez (1980) shows, in effect, that stagnation in peasant output was even more dramatic during 1967–77.

8 Economic crisis and the peasant economy, 1975–1980

1 Given that Peru is a net importer of capital, its balance of services always shows deficit. Hence, the surplus in the balance of trade is crucial to maintain long-run external equilibrium in the economy.

2 Clearly the burden of the crisis did not fall on capitalists; on the contrary, it seems that the crisis was very profitable for them. For the case of commercial banks, for instance, the average rate of profit jumped from 15.9% in 1975 to 22.5% in 1979 (*Latin American Regional Report. The Andean Group*, 23 January 1981, p. 5).

3 As anticipated by these arguments, the results obtained with this policy were not satisfactory and the government cut the program by the end of 1981.

4 At the present time the consumption of urban goods is decreasing in favor of a return to goods produced in the community, as in the case of substitution of animal fat for cooking oil, of treebark (of the *taxana*, for example) for soaps and detergents, roof-tiles in place of corrugated iron and transport by foot rather than in trucks. In reference to these substitutions, one effect of the market exchange has rarely been noted: in this process the traditional technology is lost. In the present period of crisis the peasants desire to return to their traditional technology, but in many cases it has already been lost.

9 Conclusions: reality, theory and policy

1 In this discussion one should include cooperative enterprises as well as capitalist enterprises to be more precise with regard to the organizational form of modern enterprises in Peru in the Post-Agrarian Reform period. Nonetheless, the argument is equally valid in the case of the cooperative enterprise, as its economic behavior with respect to permanent and seasonal employment is not very different from that of the capitalist enterprise. For a theoretical analysis, see Caballero (1978).

2 Foods processed in the communities have given way to urban products, as in the case of *chicha* replaced by beer. In textiles and manufacture, the peasants' clothing now shows a greater urban influence – synthetic fabrics in place of their own production of wool (woolen manufactures). The difference between generations is remarkable among the peasants; only the older people wear clothing made mainly of wool. Products made of plastic have invaded the countryside, displacing wool, as in the case of sacks and ropes, and native ceramics – pots, containers and cooking utensils.

Bibliography

Alvarez, Elena (1980). *Política Agraria y Estancamiento de la Agricultura, 1969–1977*. Lima: Instituto de Estudios Peruanos.

Baer, Werner and Figueroa, Adolfo (1981). 'Equity and State Enterprises: Some Reflections Based on the Cases of Brazil and Peru', in T. Bruneau and P. Faucher (eds), *Authoritarian Capitalism: Brazil's Contemporary Economic and Political Development*. Boulder: Westview Press.

Caballero, José M. (1978). 'Los Eventuales en las Cooperativas Costeñas Peruanas: Un Modelo Analítico'. *Economía* (Lima), Vol. I.

Caballero, José M. and Alvarez, Elena (1980). *Aspectos Cuantitativos de la Reforma Agraria, 1969–1979*. Lima: Instituto de Estudios Peruanos.

Cotlear, Daniel (1979). *El Sistema de Enganche a Principios del Siglo XX: Una Versión Diferente*. Bachelor's thesis in Economics. Lima: Universidad Católica.

de Janvry, Alain (1974). 'The Political Economy of Rural Development in Latin America: an Interpretation'. *American Journal of Agricultural Economics*, Vol. 57.

Donges, Juergen (1979). 'The Economic Model Order at the Crossroad: Past Development Trends, the Commodities Problem, and North–South Trade Rules'. Published in Spanish version in J. Donges *et al.*, *América Latina y la Economía Mundial*. Buenos Aires: Instituto Torcuato Di Tella.

Figueroa, Adolfo (1974). *Estructura del Consumo y Distribución de Ingresos en Lima Metropolitana, 1968–1969*. Lima: Universidad Católica.

Figueroa, Adolfo (1975). 'The Impact of Current Reforms on Income Distribution in Peru', in A. Foxley (ed.), *Income Distribution in Latin America*. Cambridge, Eng.: Cambridge University Press.

Figueroa, Adolfo (1976). *El Empleo Rural en el Perú*. Geneva: ILO (mimeo).

Figueroa, Adolfo (1978). 'La Economía de las Comunidades Campesinas: El Caso de la Sierra Sur del Perú', in E. Valencia *et al.*, *Campesinado e Indigenismo en América Latina*. Lima: Ediciones CELTAS.

Figueroa, Adolfo (1981). 'Agricultural Price Policy and Rural Incomes in Peru'. *Quarterly Review of Economics and Business*, Vol. 21, No. 3.

Figueroa, Adolfo (1982). *Reestructuración Agraria en la Sierra Peruana*. Lima: Confederación Campesina del Perú, Escuelas Campesinas, No. 1.

Hayami, Yujiro and Ruttan, Vernon (1971). *Agricultural Development: An International Perspective*. Baltimore: The Johns Hopkins Press.

Hopkins, Raul (1981). *Desarrollo Desigual y Crisis en la Agricultura Peruana, 1944–1969*. Lima: Instituto de Estudios Peruanos.

Hunt, Shane (1975). 'Direct Foreign Investment in Peru: New Rules for an Old Game', in A. Lowenthal (ed.), *The Peruvian Experiment: Continuity and Change under Military Rule*. Princeton: Princeton University Press.

Hymer, Stephen and Resnick, Stephen (1969). 'A Model of an Agrarian Economy with Non Agricultural Activities'. *American Economic Review*, Vol. LIX, September.

Lajo, Manuel (1979). 'Industria Agroalimentaria y Transnacionales: El Caso Peruano'. Publicaciones CISEPA, No. 43. Lima: Universidad Católica.

Musgrove, Philip (1978). *Consumer Behavior in Latin America, Income and Spending of Families in Ten Andean Cities*. Washington: The Brookings Institution.

Okun, Arthur (1975). *Equality and Efficiency. The Big Trade-Off*. Washington: The Brookings Institution.

Pulgar Vidal, Javier (1972). *Geografía del Perú*. Lima: Editorial Universo.

Quijano, Anibal (1968). 'Tendencies in Peruvian Development and in the Class Structure', in J. Petras and M. Zeitlin (eds), *Latin America: Reform or Revolution*. New York: Fawcett.

Roemer, Michael (1970). *Fishing for Growth: Export-led Development in Peru, 1950–1967*. Cambridge, Mass.: Harvard University Press.

Ruiz, Liliana (1980). *Términos de Intercambio Campo-Ciudad*. Bachelor's thesis in Economics. Lima: Universidad Católica.

Schultz, Theodore (1964). *Transforming Traditional Agriculture*. New Haven: Yale University Press.

Thorp, Rosemary and Bertram, Geoffrey (1978). *Peru 1890–1975: Growth and Policy in an Open Economy*. London: Macmillan Press.

UN–CEPAL (1978). *Series Históricas del Crecimiento de América Latina*. Santiago.

Vega, Gabriela (1979). *Migración de Retorno a las Comunidades Campesinas*. Bachelor's thesis in Sociology. Lima: Universidad Católica.

Webb, Richard (1977). *Government Policy and the Distribution of Income in Peru, 1963–1973*. Cambridge, Mass.: Harvard University Press.

Webb, Richard (1981). 'Aspectos Económicos de los Subsidios al Consumo', speech of the President of the Central Bank of Peru in the Symposium on *Nutrition and Food Subsidies*. Lima: January (mimeo).

Wiesskoff, Richard and Figueroa, Adolfo (1977). 'Viewing Income Pyramids in Latin America'. *Latin America Research Review*, Vol. XI.

Statistical sources

Instituto de Planificación (1973). *Relaciones Interindustriales de la Economía Peruana*. Lima.

Oficina Nacional de Estadísticas y Censos (1970). *Anuario Estadístico del Perú*. Lima.

Oficina Nacional de Estadísticas y Censos (1975). *Censo de Población, 1972*.

Banco Central de Reserva. *Memorias* (1974–9); *Reseña Económica* (1981) and *Cuentas Nacionales 1950–1974*.

Ministerio de Trabajo (1981). *Situación Ocupacional Cuarto Trimestre 1980*. Lima: February.

Index

CAMBRIDGE LATIN AMERICAN STUDIES

Cambridge Latin American Studies